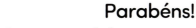

plurall

Parabéns!
Agora você faz parte do **Plurall**, a plataforma digital do seu livro didático!
Acesse e conheça todos os recursos e funcionalidades disponíveis para as suas aulas digitais.

Baixe o aplicativo do **Plurall** para Android e IOS ou acesse **www.plurall.net** e cadastre-se utilizando o seu código de acesso exclusivo:

CB027827

AAAJMWKA9

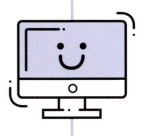

Este é o seu código de acesso Plurall.
Cadastre-se e ative-o para ter acesso aos conteúdos relacionados a esta obra.

 @plurallnet

 @plurallnetoficial

SOMOS
EDUCAÇÃO

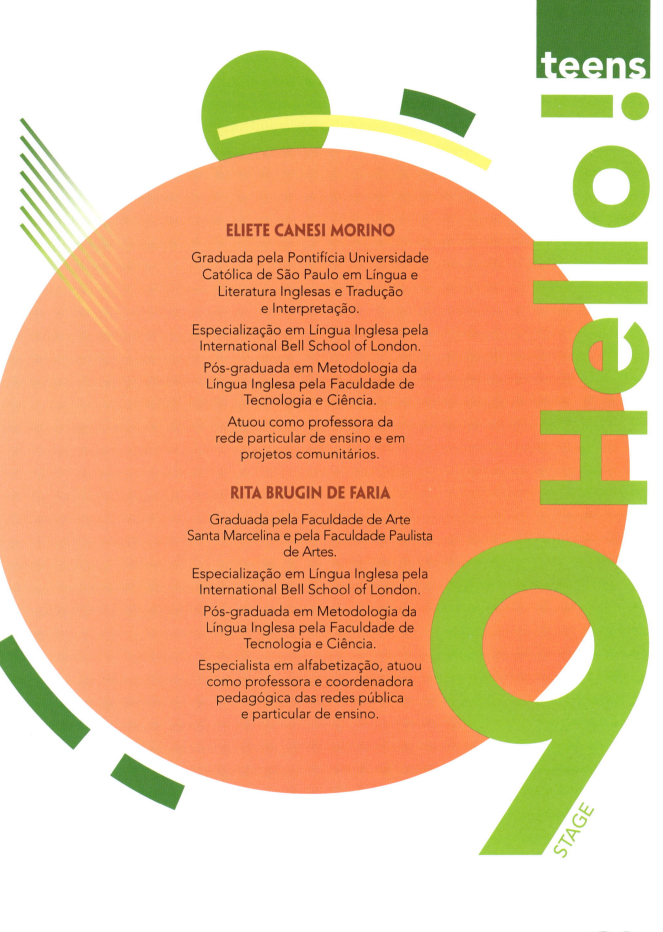

ELIETE CANESI MORINO

Graduada pela Pontifícia Universidade Católica de São Paulo em Língua e Literatura Inglesas e Tradução e Interpretação.

Especialização em Língua Inglesa pela International Bell School of London.

Pós-graduada em Metodologia da Língua Inglesa pela Faculdade de Tecnologia e Ciência.

Atuou como professora da rede particular de ensino e em projetos comunitários.

RITA BRUGIN DE FARIA

Graduada pela Faculdade de Arte Santa Marcelina e pela Faculdade Paulista de Artes.

Especialização em Língua Inglesa pela International Bell School of London.

Pós-graduada em Metodologia da Língua Inglesa pela Faculdade de Tecnologia e Ciência.

Especialista em alfabetização, atuou como professora e coordenadora pedagógica das redes pública e particular de ensino.

teens

Hello!

9 STAGE

editora ática

editora ática

Direção Presidência: Mario Ghio Júnior

Direção de Conteúdo e Operações: Wilson Troque

Direção editorial: Luiz Tonolli e Lidiane Vivaldini Olo

Gestão de projeto editorial: Mirian Senra

Gestão de área: Alice Silvestre

Coordenação: Renato Malkov

Edição: Ana Lucia Militello, Carla Fernanda Nascimento (assist.), Caroline Santos, Danuza Dias Gonçalves, Maiza Prande Bernardello, Milena Rocha (assist.), Sabrina Cairo Bileski

Planejamento e controle de produção: Patrícia Eiras e Adjane Queiroz

Revisão: Hélia de Jesus Gonsaga (ger.), Kátia Scaff Marques (coord.), Rosângela Muricy (coord.), Ana Curci, Ana Maria Herrera, Ana Paula C. Malfa, Arali Gomes, Diego Carbone, Gabriela M. Andrade, Kátia S. Lopes Godoi, Luís M. Boa Nova, Patricia Cordeiro, Paula T. de Jesus; Amanda T. Silva e Bárbara de M. Genereze (estagiárias)

Arte: Daniela Amaral (ger.), Catherine Saori Ishihara (coord.) e Letícia Lavôr (edit. arte)

Diagramação: Estúdio Lima

Iconografia e tratamento de imagem: Sílvio Kligin (ger.), Claudia Bertolazzi (coord.), Célia Rosa (pesquisa iconográfica), Fernanda Crevin (tratamento)

Licenciamento de conteúdos de terceiros: Thiago Fontana (coord.), Flavia Zambon e Angra Marques (licenciamento de textos), Erika Ramires, Luciana Pedrosa Bierbauer, Luciana Cardoso Sousa e Claudia Rodrigues (analistas adm.)

Ilustrações: Fido Nesti e Filipe Rocha

Cartografia: Eric Fuzii (coord.), Robson Rosendo da Rocha (edit. arte)

Design: Gláucia Koller (ger.), Talita Guedes (proj. gráfico e capa) e Gustavo Vanini (assist. arte)

Foto de capa: Uwe Umstätter/Westend61/Getty Images

Dados Internacionais de Catalogação na Publicação (CIP)

```
Morino, Eliete Canesi
   Hello teens 9º ano / Eliete Canesi Morino, Rita Brugin
de Faria. - 8. ed. - São Paulo : Ática, 2019.

   Suplementado pelo manual do professor.
   Bibliografia.
   ISBN: 978-85-08-19356-1 (aluno)
   ISBN: 978-85-08-19357-8 (professor)


   1.   Língua inglesa (Ensino fundamental). I. Faria,
Rita Brugin de. II. Título.


2019-0180                        CDD: 372.652
```

Julia do Nascimento - Bibliotecária - CRB-8/010142

2023
Código da obra CL 742205
CAE 654385 (AL) / 654386 (PR)
8ª edição
4ª impressão
De acordo com a BNCC.

Impressão e acabamento: EGB Editora Gráfica Bernardi Ltda.

Uma publicação

WELCOME, STUDENTS, TO HELLO! TEENS 9

Hello!

A língua inglesa está cada vez mais presente no nosso dia a dia. Ela chega até nós por intermédio dos mais diversos canais de comunicação e, assim, a todo momento estamos ouvindo, lendo e falando espontaneamente em inglês.

Em virtude da evolução da tecnologia, as distâncias tornaram-se virtuais e o inglês é o idioma mais utilizado por pessoas de diferentes nacionalidades que querem se comunicar entre si.

A **Coleção Hello! Teens**, escrita para você, um adolescente do mundo contemporâneo, quer motivá-lo a aprender inglês por meio de temas instigantes associados a atividades que facilitarão sua aprendizagem.

Participe ativamente das aulas refletindo e interagindo com seus colegas e desfrute de todos os benefícios que esta aprendizagem pode lhe proporcionar!

As autoras

CONTENTS

	WORD WORK	FOCUS ON LANGUAGE	LISTEN AND SPEAK	READ AND WRITE	TIPS FOR LIFE
WELCOME! P. 6	Content review from Hello! Teens 8				
UNIT 1 Amazing Languages P. 10	Adjectives to express feelings and emotions	Review: simple present, simple past (regular verbs), simple future with will, present continuous, past continuous, future with going to Some, any and no (compound words)	Interview with an animal communicator Interview a classmate	Text 1: ASL fingerspelling alphabet Text 2: Almanac article Create a classroom almanac	Inclusion
UNIT 2 I Enjoy Extreme Sports P. 26	Extreme sports	Modal verbs: can, may, might, could, would Tag questions	Advertisement Expressing opinion	Text 1: Article Text 2: Comic strips Create comic strips	Safety in extreme sports
REVIEW	**Units 1 and 2 - p. 42 and 43**				
UNIT 3 You Must Turn Your Phone Off! P. 44	On-line activities and devices	Review: subject pronouns, possessive adjectives, possessive pronouns Modal verbs: should, must, mustn't	Public Service Announcement (PSA) Group oral presentation	Text 1: Article Text 2: Research Produce a graph	Internet safety
UNIT 4 Keep Fit, Keep Healthy P. 60	Fitness and exercising vocabulary, sports equipment	Relative clauses and relative pronouns (who/that, which/that, whose), Review: subject and object pronouns Used to	Informative video Ask and answer questions	Text 1: Quiz Text 2: Flyer Create a flyer	Physical and mental safety
REVIEW	**Units 3 and 4 - p. 76 and 77**				

	WORD WORK	FOCUS ON LANGUAGE	LISTEN AND SPEAK	READ AND WRITE	TIPS FOR LIFE
UNIT 5 What Is Genetics? P. 78	Biology and genetics vocabulary	Definite article (the), indefinite article (a/an), relative pronouns (who, that, which, whose, where), linking words	Oral presentation and news report Group discussion	Text 1: News article Text 2: Cartoons Text 3: Article Create a questionnaire	Ethics in life
UNIT 6 Relationships P. 94	Feelings and emotions	Present perfect, time adverbs (ever, never, already, just, yet)	Dialogs Group discussion	Text 1: Quotes Text 2: Acrostic poem Create an acrostic poem	Relationship and respect

REVIEW — **Units 5 and 6** - p. 110 and 111

	WORD WORK	FOCUS ON LANGUAGE	LISTEN AND SPEAK	READ AND WRITE	TIPS FOR LIFE
UNIT 7 Thinking of Global Issues P. 112	Health, social and environmental issues	Present perfect with for and since, present perfect x simple past, active x passive voice	News report Dialog	Text 1: Infographic Text 2: News report Write a news report	Global issues
UNIT 8 Let's Save Our Planet! P. 128	Green practices	First and second conditionals, false cognates (false friends)	List Group discussion and oral presentation	Text 1: News report Text 2: Comic strip Text 3: Song lyrics Write song lyrics	Respect and preserve the environment

REVIEW — **Units 7 and 8** - p. 144 and 145

EXTRA PRACTICE P. 146
PROJECTS P. 154
FUN ACTIVITIES P. 158
GLOSSARY P. 162

IRREGULAR VERBS P. 166
GRAMMAR HELPER P. 167
WORKBOOK P. 177

WELCOME!

ON THE SCREEN

◀1 Read the poster and check.

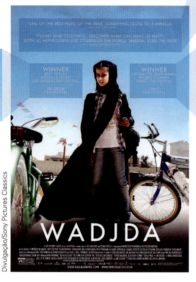

"ONE OF THE BEST FILMS OF THE YEAR. SOMETHING CLOSE TO A MIRACLE."
– Oliver Lyttelton, THE PLAYLIST

"FUNNY AND TOUCHING. DISCOVER WHAT CAN MAKE US HAPPY, BOTH AS MOVIEGOERS AND CITIZENS OF THE WORLD. 'WADJDA' DOES THE TRICK."
– Joe Morgenstern, WALL STREET JOURNAL

WINNER
BEST PICTURE
AUDIENCE AWARD
LOS ANGELES FILM FESTIVAL

TELLURIDE
FILM FESTIVAL

WINNER
CINEMA FOR PEACE AWARD
INTERFILM AWARD
VENICE FILM FESTIVAL

TRIBECA
FILM FESTIVAL

a. ○ *Wadjda* is a theater play.

b. ○ *Wadjda* was awarded international prizes.

c. ○ *Wadjda* is a movie.

d. ○ There are two positive reviews about *Wadjda* in the poster.

◀2 Read the storyline and answer the questions in your notebook.

www.imdb.com/title/tt2258858/plotsummary?ref_=tt_stry_pl

Storyline

WADJDA is a 10-year-old girl living in a suburb of Riyadh, the capital of Saudi Arabia. Although she lives in a conservative world, Wadjda is fun loving, entrepreneurial and always pushing the boundaries of what she can get away with. After a fight with her friend Abdullah, a neighborhood boy she shouldn't be playing with, Wadjda sees a beautiful green bicycle for sale. She wants the bicycle desperately so that she can beat Abdullah in a race. But Wadjda's mother won't allow it, fearing repercussions from a society that sees bicycles as dangerous to a girl's virtue. So Wadjda decides to try and raise the money herself. At first, Wadjda's mother is too preoccupied with convincing her husband not to take a second wife to realize what's going on. And soon enough Wadjda's plans are thwarted when she is caught running various schemes at school. Just as she is losing hope of raising enough money, she hears of a cash prize for a *Quran* recitation competition at her school. She devotes herself to the memorization and recitation of *Quranic* verses, and her teachers begin to see Wadjda as a model pious girl. The competition isn't going to be easy, especially for a troublemaker like Wadjda, but she refuses to give in. She is determined to continue fighting for her dreams.

— *Written by Razor Film Produktion GmbH*

Available at: <www.imdb.com/title/tt2258858/plotsummary?ref_=tt_stry_pl>. Accessed on: Mar. 12, 2019.

a. Who is Wadjda? What is her main objective?

b. Based on the text, list some words that describe Wadjda's personality.

c. Why didn't her mother allow her to buy a bicycle?

d. How does the movie end? Use your imagination and write a possible ending for it.

TO LEARN MORE

Watch the official movie trailer in: <www.youtube.com/watch?v=3koigluYOH0>.
You can also watch an interview with the movie director, Haifaa Al Mansour, available at:
<www.youtube.com/watch?v=q3q05VLc6u4>. Accessed on: Apr. 11, 2019.

SIMPLE PAST × PAST CONTINUOUS

3 Choose the correct options from the box to complete the sentences.

> their parents arrived   we left the party   Jonas scared her   I arrived

a. They were watching a movie when _____.

b. I didn't get the explanation. The teacher was giving the last instructions when _____.

c. Kitty was reading a book when _____.

d. It was raining a lot when _____.

4 Read the sentences from activity 3 again. Underline the periods in the Simple Past and circle the periods in the Past Continuous.

5 Check the true sentences about the use of Simple Past and Past Continuous.

a. ◯ We use the Simple Past to talk about actions that happened and finished at some point in the past.

b. ◯ We use the Simple Past to talk about continuous actions in the present.

c. ◯ We use the Past Continuous to talk about actions that started in the past and are still happening today.

d. ◯ We use the Past Continuous to talk about actions that were occurring in the past until some point of interruption.

e. ◯ We use the Simple Past and the Past Continuous indistinctly.

6 Look at the pictures and complete the sentences.

a. He was walking and looking at his cell phone at the same time when _____.

b. _____ when the phone rang.

c. She was playing the guitar when

_____.

Ilustrações: Filipe Rocha/ Arquivo da editora

7 Look at the pictures and write sentences using the adjectives from the box. Follow the example.

fast	sad	slow	happy	old	crowded	empty	new

a.

The red car is running fast, but the silver car is going slow.

b.

_____

_____

c.

_____

_____

8 Write comparative sentences using the information from activity 7. Follow the example.

a. The red car is faster than the silver one./The silver car is slower than the red one.

b. _____

c. _____

9 Unscramble the sentences.

a. are/the/fastest/cheetahs/Earth/on/animals/land.

_____

b. the/animal/is/tallest/the/giraffe/the/in/zoo.

_____

c. most/the/the/part/the/body/brain/is/of/important.

_____

PREFIXES AND SUFFIXES

10 Match the root words to the correct prefix or suffix. Then complete the sentences using the new words you created.

Root words					
usual	legible	respect	play	help	friend

Prefixes and suffixes					
dis	un	ship	il	ful	re

a. Never _____ your teachers. They are precious!

b. Thanks for being present. Our _____ will last forever!

c. This work of art has an _____ caption.

d. Parents usually don't go on school field trips. It's _____.

e. I didn't see the goal. Can you _____ the video, please?

f. Could you tell me where the restaurant is, please? It would be very _____.

FUTURE TENSE

11 Look at the pictures and make your own predictions about the future. Follow the example.

a.

Petr Akulin/Shutterstock

Personal flights will be common./
Personal flights won't be common.

b.
Ingo Wagner/picture-alliance/dpa/
Associated Press/Glow Images

_____

c.

Ryumin Alexander/Zuma Press/Fotoarena

_____

d.

BSIP/UIG/Getty Images

_____

12 Describe your plans for this year as an English student. What would you like to accomplish? How are you going to do that? Write the answer in your notebook.

AMAZING LANGUAGES

Hero Images/Getty Images

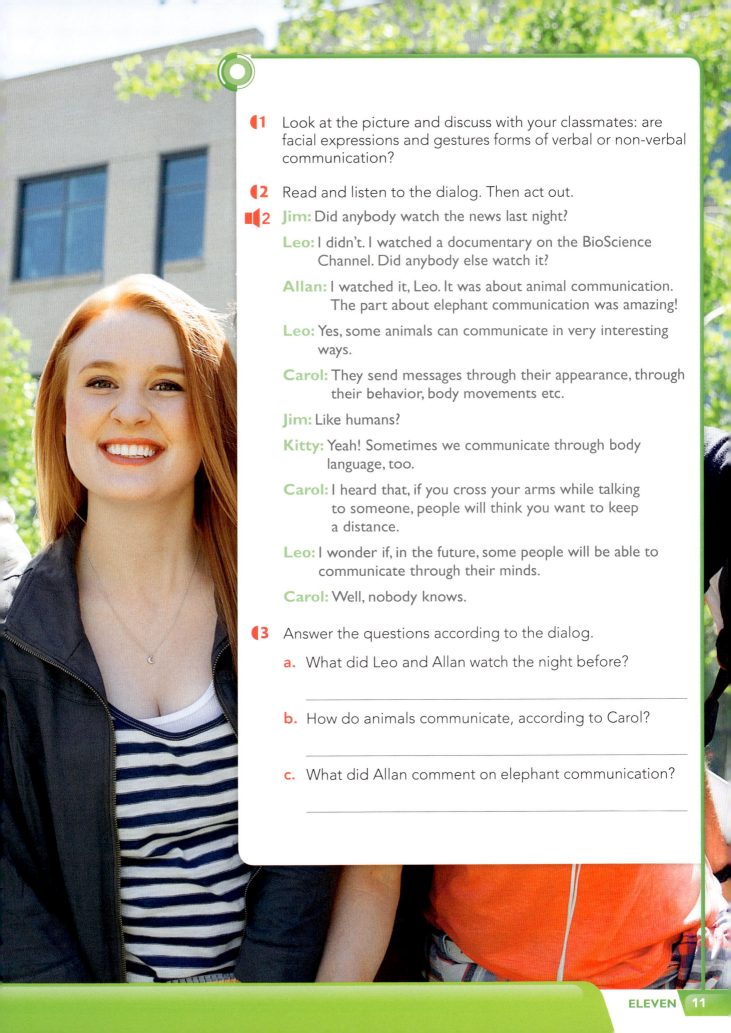

1 Look at the picture and discuss with your classmates: are facial expressions and gestures forms of verbal or non-verbal communication?

2 Read and listen to the dialog. Then act out.

Jim: Did anybody watch the news last night?

Leo: I didn't. I watched a documentary on the BioScience Channel. Did anybody else watch it?

Allan: I watched it, Leo. It was about animal communication. The part about elephant communication was amazing!

Leo: Yes, some animals can communicate in very interesting ways.

Carol: They send messages through their appearance, through their behavior, body movements etc.

Jim: Like humans?

Kitty: Yeah! Sometimes we communicate through body language, too.

Carol: I heard that, if you cross your arms while talking to someone, people will think you want to keep a distance.

Leo: I wonder if, in the future, some people will be able to communicate through their minds.

Carol: Well, nobody knows.

3 Answer the questions according to the dialog.

a. What did Leo and Allan watch the night before?

_____

b. How do animals communicate, according to Carol?

_____

c. What did Allan comment on elephant communication?

_____

THINKING AHEAD

1 Read the title of the text and the definition in the first paragraph. In pairs, think of some examples of body language you use.

https://www.nacada.ksu.edu/Resources/Clearinghouse/View-Articles/Body-Language-Around-the-World.aspx

Body Language Around the World

by: Kris Rugsaken | Advising Center Coordinator. Ball State University

Definition: 'Body language' includes all the communication through the non-verbal channel. This can include how we greet others, how we sit or stand, our facial expressions, our clothes, hair styles, tone of voice, eye movements, how we listen, how we breathe, how close we stand to others, and how we touch others. […]

Understanding Body Language

[…] This article will give a few examples of how body parts […] are used for communicating in different parts of the world.

In most societies, a nodding head signifies agreement or approval. But in some cultures, like parts of Greece, Bulgaria and Turkey, a nodding head means 'no.' […]

While good eye contact is praised and expected in the West, it is seen as a sign of disrespect and challenge in other cultures, including Asian and African. […]

In some cultures, such as Filipino, Native American, Puerto Rican, and several Latin American, people use their lips to point, instead of a finger.

Handshaking is the common form of greeting and leave taking in the Western culture. While it is being accepted in Asia, the Asians still prefer a different form of greeting: a bow in East Asia, a 'wai' (joining the two hands together like in prayer) for some Southern and Southeastern Asian countries. Asians and Middle Easterners prefer a soft handshake. Strong grips are interpreted as a sign of aggression.

Sitting cross-legged is common in North America and some European countries but it is viewed as disrespectful in Asia and the Middle East. […]

Available at: <https://www.nacada.ksu.edu/Resources/Clearinghouse/View-Articles/Body-Language-Around-the-World.aspx>. Accessed on: Mar. 10, 2019.

2 Look at the images and write one or two words to describe the meanings expressed by these gestures.

a — Japan

b — Greece

c — Saudi Arabia

d — Philippines

Ilustrações: Filipe Rocha/ Arquivo da editora

_____ _____ _____ _____

3 Why do you think the meaning of gestures and expressions change depending on the culture? Talk to your teacher and classmates.

TO LEARN MORE

Watch some body language techniques at: <www.youtube.com/watch?v=TD884Dl-kLc>. Accessed on: Feb. 21, 2019.

WORD WORK

1 Observe the expressions in the pictures. These people are...

happy

sad

angry

worried

disappointed

surprised

sleepy

tired

cold

impatient

frightened

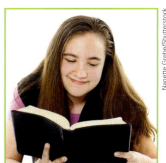

interested

2 Look at the pictures and read about each situation. Then complete the sentences with words from activity 1.

a. It's late. Kitty and Leo didn't get home. John is

_____ about them.

b. Bob loves watching movies with his family,

but last night he was _____

because he was not _____ in the movie.

c. Helen loves to teach. And she really likes her students. But yesterday she was very

_____ with them because everybody was talking a lot.

• Now complete the sentences with information about yourself.

 I'm in a good mood when _____.

I'm in a bad mood when _____.

3 Do you believe that pets have a special way of communicating with their owners? If you have a pet, explain if it asks you for food or something else.

4 Look at the pictures and answer: What's the dog "saying" to you? It is…

a

submissive
furious

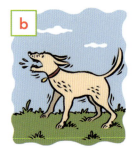
b

playfull
aggressive

c

scared
calm

d

depressed
alert

TIME FOR A GAME

Let's play **Stop** and **Hangman**!

FOCUS ON LANGUAGE

1 Read these sentences from the dialog and match them with the correct verb tenses descriptions.

a. **Leo:** I **watched** a documentary on the BioScience Channel.

b. **Kitty:** We **communicate** through body language, too.

c. **Leo:** Some people will **be able** to communicate through their minds.

GRAMMAR HELPER

Go to page 167.

○ It talks about a prediction for the future, it is in the Simple Future.

○ It expresses a past action, it is in the Simple Past.

○ It talks about a general truth; it is in the Simple Present.

2 Read the charts below and complete them with the missing information. Add your own examples.

Simple Present	
Affirmative	My dog always **greets** people by giving them her left paw. _____
Interrogative	**Do** you **work** with animals? _____
Negative	She **doesn't want** to talk anymore. Look at her face. _____

Simple Past – Regular Verbs		
Most verbs + **ed** ask → asked	Verbs ending in **e** + **d** use → used	Verbs ending in **consonant** + **y** – **y** → **i** + **ed** worry → worried

Example sentences:

_____

_____

Simple Future	
Affirmative	I **will study** Libras, the Brazilian sign language. _____
Interrogative	**Will** she **bring** us that book about animal communication? _____
Negative	We **won't watch** any documentary. We are too tired. _____

3 In pairs, complete the sentences with the Simple Present, Simple Past or Simple Future of the verbs given.

a. She _____ me for help when I _____. (ask – arrive)

b. My father _____ the house yesterday. (clean up)

c. Mike and Janet _____ how to do their homework. (not – know)

d. You look worried. Is it because of the test? Don't worry, I _____ you. (help)

4 Read the comic strip and discuss the questions in pairs.

a. Why does Earl, the grandpa, think it's good to wear the same shirt every day? Do you agree with him? Why (not)?

b. Observe the highlighted words in the comic strip and answer.

- Which part of the sentence refers to an action that was happening in the past (Past Continuous)?

- Which part refers to an action that is ongoing in the present time (Present Continuous)?

GRAMMAR HELPER

Go to page 168.

5 Read the chart and add your own examples.

Present Continuous		
Affirmative	**Interrogative**	**Negative**
I'm trying to communicate with my dog.	**Are** you **watching** the interview with the animal communicator?	**They** are **not arguing**, mom.
_____	_____	_____

Past Continuous		
Affirmative	**Interrogative**	**Negative**
I'm sure my hamster **was trying** to say something to me when I fed him yesterday.	What **were** they **doing** this morning?	She **wasn't talking** to me.
_____	_____	_____

6 Read the cartoon and answer: why does the dog keep barking to his slippers? Then read the speech bubble and choose the most appropriate option.

a. ◯ A future action that always happen.

b. ◯ A planned action/intention for the future.

c. ◯ A prediction for the future based on an opinion.

7 Read the box and complete it with the missing information. Add your own examples.

Future with going to		
Subject	**Verb To Be**	**Going To + Main Verb**
I	_____	(not) _____ play in the backyard.
You	_____	_____
He/She/It	_____	_____
We/You/They	_____	_____

Example sentence: _____

8 Joe Navarro is always busy. Describe his schedule for next week using the verbs given in the appropriate form.

a. On Monday, _____. (attend/international conference)

b. On Tuesday, _____. (visit/Brit offices)

c. On Wednesday, _____. (open/new Brit factory)

d. On Thursday, _____. (meet/President of the Common Market)

e. On Friday, _____. (speak/Dutch Minister of Technology)

9 Write sentences with the words given using the appropriate verb tenses.

a. in the future/their pets/talk/everybody/I think

_____

b. Amanda and Carlo/tomorrow;/visit the vet/their rabbit/be/depressed/

_____

c. when I/feed Fluffy/yesterday/she be not/interested/anymore/I notice/in her food

_____

d. to her turtle now/try to talk/seem to understand/Melissa/but he not/her.

_____

10 Read the following sentences from the dialog and the chart below. Then complete the chart with the missing information.

Jim: Did **anybody** watch the news last night?

Carol: Well, **nobody** knows.

Some, any and no (compound words)		
People	**Things**	**Places**
somebody/someone	_____	somewhere
anybody/_____	anything	_____
_____/no one	_____	nowhere

11 Complete the sentences using compound words.

a. When _____ raises their eyebrows, they're probably surprised or shocked at _____.

b. Please, don't interrupt _____ who is talking.

c. _____ was paying attention, because they all looked bored.

d. Your body language tells a lot, you can hide

_____.

LANGUAGE TIPS

nothing/nobody/no one/ nowhere
These words are used in positive sentences, but they have a negative meaning. Compare:
I have **nothing** to say./I don't have **anything** to say.

GRAMMAR HELPER

Go to page 169.

LISTEN AND SPEAK

1 You are going to listen to an interview with Anna Breytenbach, an animal communicator. Read the introductory text and answer: what does she do in her profession?

> Anna Breytenbach is a professional animal communicator trained through the Assisi International Animal Institute in California and has been practicing over a decade in South Africa, Europe and the USA. Her conversation experience includes working with various wild animals in educational and rehabilitation programs.
>
> AFTERNOON Express. *Animal Communicator Tells All*. Available at: <https://www.youtube.com/watch?v=K6DRxXk4Qks> (0:00–0:20). Accessed on: Feb. 24, 2019.

_____

_____

2 Listen to the interview and check the information you hear.

4 a. ◯ Anna explains what an animal communicator does.

b. ◯ She talks about the types of animals she works with.

c. ◯ She briefly describes the process used to communicate with an animal.

d. ◯ She explains how she started communicating with animals in the past.

3 Listen to the first question again and underline the correct word.

5 She compares the work of an animal communicator to a *psychologist / translator / veterinarian*.

4 Listen to the second question and check the image that best describes the process of communicating with animals according to Anna Breytenbach.

a.
Jaromir Chalabala/Shutterstock

b.
Serhii Bobyk/Shutterstock

c.
Kzenon/Shutterstock

5 Listen to the third question and write **T** (true) or **F** (false) for each statement.

7
a. ◯ The interviewer (Bonnie) thinks it is a gift that Anna has.

b. ◯ Anna explains that she discovered this gift when she was eleven.

c. ◯ Anna says that this is a process that anyone can do.

d. ◯ According to Anna, in the past, people usually communicated with animals.

e. ◯ Anna says that nowadays humans are very busy and don't pay attention to their intuition.

f. ◯ According to Anna, we are educated to communicate with animals, but we don't practice it.

6 Do you think that anyone can develop a skill to communicate with animals? Why (not)? Talk to your classmates and teacher.

7 In pairs, you are going to interview each other for the school's webpage or blog/vlog.
8 First, listen to the interview again paying attention to its structure.

a. Observe how the interview begins, is conducted and is concluded.

b. Decide the topic of the interview. Here you find some ideas, but you can choose other subjects, such as:

- Your opinion about animal communication.

- Your relationship with your pets and other animals.

- What you know about human body language and how it affects communication etc.

c. Create three to four questions and write them down in your notebook if necessary.

PRONUNCIATION CORNER

1 Listen and act out the jazz chant.

9
A: Hey Timothy. What's up?

B: Everything is OK, thanks.

A: Tell me Timothy, how's your brother Theo?

B: Fine. We are thinking about going to the theater.
Are you free for the theater next Thursday?

A: I'm free, we are in three.

B: You mean... three tickets...

A: Yes, three tickets for three.

A: I'll try to go today to the theater...

B: ... and get three free tickets for three.

A: What do you think about that?

B: I think that is a fantastic idea!

2 Listen and practice.
10

think - **s**ink	**th**ank - **t**ank
then - **z**en	**th**ey - **d**ay
three - **f**ree	**th**in - **f**in

READ AND WRITE

Text 1

1 Look at the image below. What is the equivalent in Portuguese for ASL (American Sign Language)?

_____

2 In which situations can you use ASL?

_____

3 Now read the text and the sentences that follows. Then check **T** (true), **F** (false) or **NM** (not mentioned).

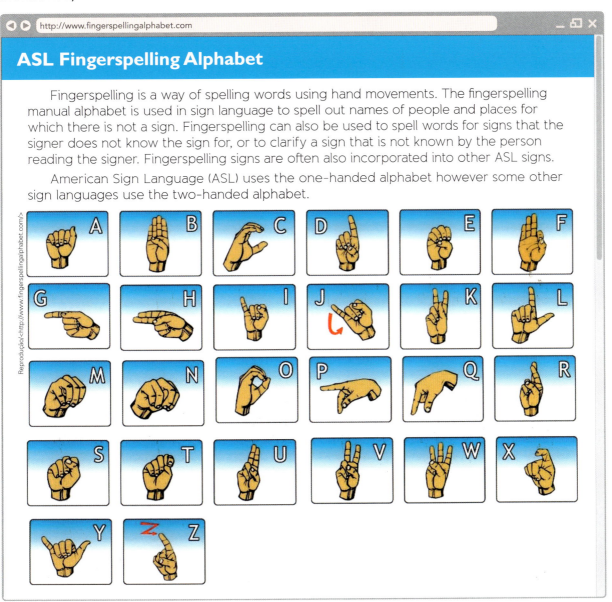

http://www.fingerspellingalphabet.com

ASL Fingerspelling Alphabet

Fingerspelling is a way of spelling words using hand movements. The fingerspelling manual alphabet is used in sign language to spell out names of people and places for which there is not a sign. Fingerspelling can also be used to spell words for signs that the signer does not know the sign for, or to clarify a sign that is not known by the person reading the signer. Fingerspelling signs are often also incorporated into other ASL signs.

American Sign Language (ASL) uses the one-handed alphabet however some other sign languages use the two-handed alphabet.

Reprodução/<http://www.fingerspellingalphabet.com/>

Available at: <http://www.fingerspellingalphabet.com/>. Accessed on: Mar. 11, 2019.

a. ◯ Fingerspelling is the process of spelling out words by using hands in precise movements.

b. ◯ To understand the communication by fingerspelling, people should pay attention to the signs and to the movements of the lips.

c. ◯ Fingerspelling can be used to spell words but not to clarify signs.

◀4 Read the question below and check the excerpt of the text that contains the answer.

> Besides using the fingerspelling manual alphabet to spell out names of people and places for which there is not a sign, which other situations can people use it?

◯ […] to spell words for signs that the signer does not know the sign for, or to clarify a sign that is not known by the person reading the signer.

◯ Fingerspelling signs are often also incorporated into other ASL signs.

◯ American Sign Language (ASL) uses the one-handed alphabet however some other sign languages use the two-handed alphabet.

◀5 Think of a sentence in English and use the ASL to say it to a classmate. Look at an example below. Take turns. Did you succeed?

Reprodução/<http://www.fingerspellingalphabet.com/>

Marcos Mesa Sam Wordley/Shutterstock

Text 2

6 Skim the text below and answer: it was extracted from...

◯ an almanac. ◯ a comic book.

Elephants get the point!

Elephants can understand the human gesture of pointing without being trained to do so, reported a team of researchers in 2013. That finding surprised many zoologists (scientists who study animals). It's long been known that domesticated animals, such as dogs, cats, horses, and even goats, can understand pointing and other human cues. But nondomesticated species of animals – including humans' closest relatives, great apes and chimps – have always failed the pointing test.

For this latest study, researchers tested 11 African elephants that regularly gave rides to tourists in the African country of Zimbabwe. None of the elephants had previously been trained to understand human gestures.

For the test, the researchers hid a snack in one of two containers. Then, in full view of each elephant, they silently pointed to the container with the food in it. The elephants went to the correct container more than two-thirds of the time. That's almost as often as 1-year-old human babies do when given a similar test!

Why do African elephants understand human pointing? The researchers think it's because the elephants already use pointing to communicate among themselves. When a wild elephant smells the odor of a nearby lion, for example, it will lift its trunk and point the tip in the direction of the smell to warn other elephants of the danger.

PHOTOCREO Michal Bednarek/Shutterstock

From: *Time for Kids Almanac 2015*. New York: Time Home Entertainment Inc., 2014. p. 25.

7 There is an important statement in the beginning of the text:

> "Elephants can understand the human gesture of pointing without being trained to do so, reported a team of researchers in 2013."

Why do you think the author of the text published this statement?

8 As you can see, the picture of the elephants occupies half of the almanac page. Why? Discuss with a classmate.

9 Check the sentences that are true about elephants.

a. ◯ Most non-domesticated species of animals have failed the pointing test.

b. ◯ Apes and chimps have succeeded the pointing test because they are humans' closest relatives.

c. ◯ African elephants gave rides to tourists.

d. ◯ The researchers also proved that elephants could be as successful as a human baby when it comes to this test.

e. ◯ Even though elephants succeed the pointing test, they do not use this ability to avoid danger.

f. ◯ The elephants in the picture are in their natural habitat.

10 Let's write texts to create your own classroom almanac! In pairs, come to an agreement
177 about the topic of your text. Then follow the steps below.

a. Do some research about the topic.

b. Look for pictures to illustrate your text. Don't forget that pictures can grab readers' attention.

c. Write a draft of your text and show it to the teacher.

d. Do all the necessary adjustments and write a final version.

e. Follow your teacher's instructions to gather all the texts to create the almanac.

_____

_____

_____

_____

_____

_____

_____

_____

_____

_____

_____

_____

_____

TIPS FOR LIFE

Inclusion

1 Read the text and discuss the following questions in pairs.

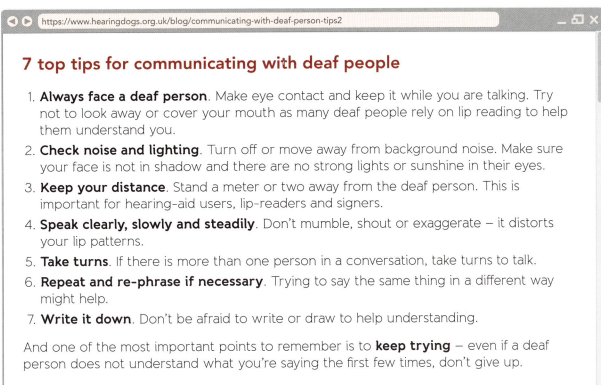

Available at: <https://www.hearingdogs.org.uk/blog/communicating-with-deaf-person-tips2/>.
Accessed on: Mar. 12, 2019.

a. Are you or do you know a deaf person? If so, do you usually follow one of these tips?

b. In your opinion, which tip is the most effective? Why?

CHECK YOUR PROGRESS	😀	😐	🙁
Languages (Body language, Libras, ASL)			
Compounds: some, any, no			
Verb tenses (review)			
Listening			
Speaking			
Reading			
Writing			

2

I ENJOY EXTREME SPORTS

Galyna Andrushko/Shutterstock

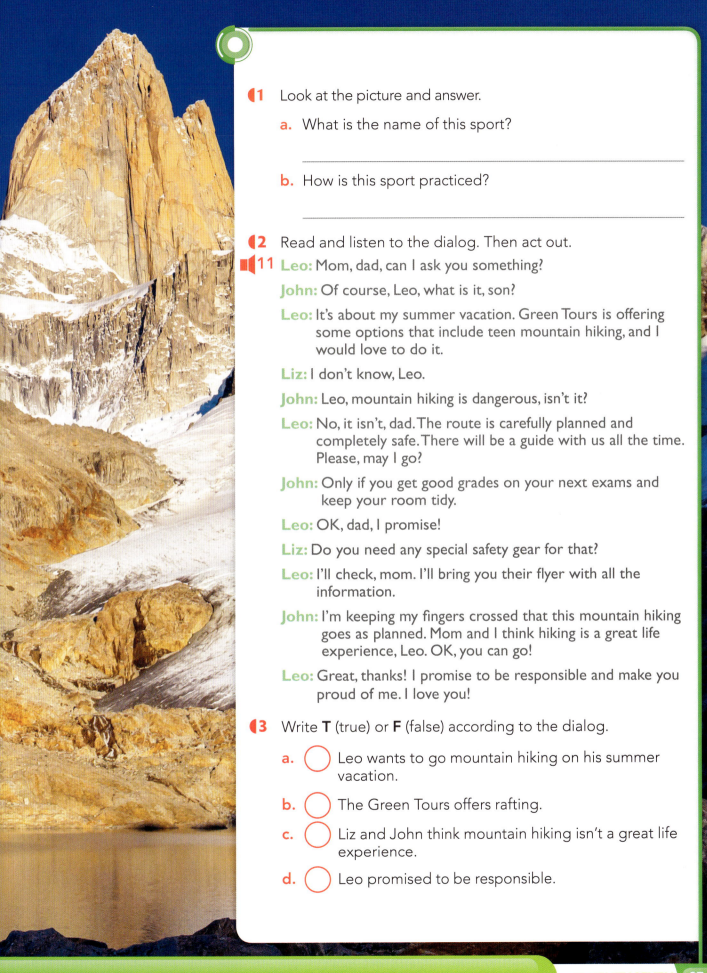

1 Look at the picture and answer.

    a. What is the name of this sport?

    _____

    b. How is this sport practiced?

    _____

2 Read and listen to the dialog. Then act out.

11

Leo: Mom, dad, can I ask you something?

John: Of course, Leo, what is it, son?

Leo: It's about my summer vacation. Green Tours is offering some options that include teen mountain hiking, and I would love to do it.

Liz: I don't know, Leo.

John: Leo, mountain hiking is dangerous, isn't it?

Leo: No, it isn't, dad. The route is carefully planned and completely safe. There will be a guide with us all the time. Please, may I go?

John: Only if you get good grades on your next exams and keep your room tidy.

Leo: OK, dad, I promise!

Liz: Do you need any special safety gear for that?

Leo: I'll check, mom. I'll bring you their flyer with all the information.

John: I'm keeping my fingers crossed that this mountain hiking goes as planned. Mom and I think hiking is a great life experience, Leo. OK, you can go!

Leo: Great, thanks! I promise to be responsible and make you proud of me. I love you!

3 Write **T** (true) or **F** (false) according to the dialog.

    a. ◯ Leo wants to go mountain hiking on his summer vacation.

    b. ◯ The Green Tours offers rafting.

    c. ◯ Liz and John think mountain hiking isn't a great life experience.

    d. ◯ Leo promised to be responsible.

1 Answer the following questions. Then talk to your classmates about them.

a. Do you like outdoor sports? Why (not)?

_____

b. Which outdoor sports are popular in your city/town?

_____

c. What do you know about hiking?

_____

2 Read the brochure about hiking and answer.

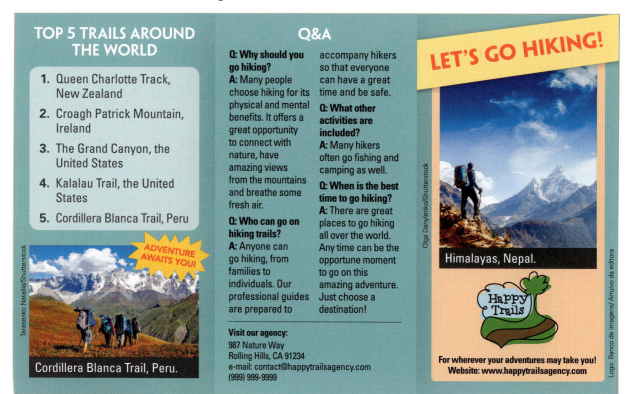

TOP 5 TRAILS AROUND THE WORLD

1. Queen Charlotte Track, New Zealand
2. Croagh Patrick Mountain, Ireland
3. The Grand Canyon, the United States
4. Kalalau Trail, the United States
5. Cordillera Blanca Trail, Peru

ADVENTURE AWAITS YOU!

Cordillera Blanca Trail, Peru.

Q&A

Q: Why should you go hiking?
A: Many people choose hiking for its physical and mental benefits. It offers a great opportunity to connect with nature, have amazing views from the mountains and breathe some fresh air.

Q: Who can go on hiking trails?
A: Anyone can go hiking, from families to individuals. Our professional guides are prepared to accompany hikers so that everyone can have a great time and be safe.

Q: What other activities are included?
A: Many hikers often go fishing and camping as well.

Q: When is the best time to go hiking?
A: There are great places to go hiking all over the world. Any time can be the opportune moment to go on this amazing adventure. Just choose a destination!

Visit our agency:
987 Nature Way
Rolling Hills, CA 91234
e-mail: contact@happytrailsagency.com
(999) 999-9999

LET'S GO HIKING!

Himalayas, Nepal.

Happy Trails

For wherever your adventures may take you!
Website: www.happytrailsagency.com

a. What countries offer the best hiking trails?

_____

b. How does this agency provide safety for hikers?

_____

c. What are the benefits of going hiking?

_____

3 Now, discuss with a classmate: was the brochure persuasive? Would you like to go hiking on any of the trails offered by this agency? Why (not)?

WORD WORK

1 Listen to some extreme sports and repeat.

🔊 **12**

watcher fox/Shutterstock

kayaking

Jan Nedbal/Shutterstock

rappelling

dcwcreations/Shutterstock

scuba diving

Panagiotis Lymperopoulos/Shutterstock

waterskiing

SvetlanaSF/Shutterstock

hang gliding

Grossinger/Shutterstock

skateboarding

homydesign/Shutterstock

surfing

maxpro/Shutterstock

mountain biking

KYTan/Shutterstock

street luging

Kulikov Aleksandr/Shutterstock

bungee jumping

windsurfing

climbing

rafting

skydiving

2 List the sports from activity 1 in the corresponding columns.

Air sports	Water sports	Land sports

3 In pairs, read the questions and discuss.

a. What extreme sport is the most exciting in your opinion?

b. Do you practice any sports? Which ones?

TIME FOR A GAME

Let's play **Mime "Where are you?"** and **Sausage Game**!

TO LEARN MORE

An extreme sport practiced by Brazilians is **sandboarding**, which consists of gliding over sand dunes with a board very similar to a snowboard. In Brazil there are wonderful places to practice this sport. On some beaches in Fortaleza, for example, there are dunes with more than 10 m in height that allow many radical maneuvers, such as the 360 degree spin, the helicopter and the backflip.

FOCUS ON LANGUAGE

1 Look at the picture and read the text paying attention to the words in **bold**.

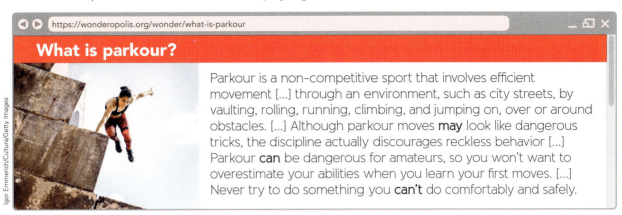

https://wonderopolis.org/wonder/what-is-parkour

What is parkour?

Parkour is a non-competitive sport that involves efficient movement [...] through an environment, such as city streets, by vaulting, rolling, running, climbing, and jumping on, over or around obstacles. [...] Although parkour moves **may** look like dangerous tricks, the discipline actually discourages reckless behavior [...] Parkour **can** be dangerous for amateurs, so you won't want to overestimate your abilities when you learn your first moves. [...] Never try to do something you **can't** do comfortably and safely.

Available at: <https://wonderopolis.org/wonder/what-is-parkour>. Accessed on: Mar. 11, 2019.

2 What are the verbs in **bold** being used for?

Go to page 169.

_____

3 Read the chart and add some examples to complete it.

Modal Verbs		
Modal	**Usage**	**Example**
Can	Permission (informal)	**Can** they participate in a bodyboarding competition?
	Request (informal)	**Can** you help me with my homework, Susan?
	Ability	
	Possibility	
May	Permission (formal)	**May** I use your computer, grandpa?
	Possibility (formal)	
Might	Possibility (formal)	I **might** start practicing some extreme sports soon.
Could	Request (formal)	**Could** you come to my office later, Ms. Williams?
	Possibility (formal)	My neighbor's dad **could** drive us to school.
	Ability	**Could** you swim when you were four years old?
Would	Offer	**Would** you like some iced tea?
	Invitation	**Would** you like to go to the movies with me next Saturday?

LANGUAGE TIPS

May and **might** can be used interchangeably to talk about possibility. Some experts believe that **might** denotes a less possible situation than **may**.

4 Read the sentences and underline the correct words to complete them.

   a. I think you're hungry. **Will/Can/Would** you like a tuna sandwich?

   b. Ms. Jones, I finished the test. **Would/May/Do** I go out now?

   c. She **might/would/do** want to learn how to surf.

   d. I'm lost. **Does/Did/Could** you show me the way home?

   e. You look tired. **Will/Can/Did** I help you?

5 Classify the use of modal verbs in **ability**, **permission**, **possibility**, **offer**, **invitation** or **request**.

   a. This orange juice is delicious. Would you like some?

   _____

   b. Can I talk to you now, Ms. Rogers?

   _____

   c. Jane didn't come to her windsurfing lesson today. She might have missed the bus.

   _____

   d. I'm going to go surfing this afternoon. Would you like to come too?

   _____

   e. Can you get the surfboard for me, please?

   _____

   f. My father can't drive a motorcycle. He thinks it's difficult.

   _____

   g. Grandma, could you lend me some money for the holidays?

   _____

6 Write four sentences using: **can**, **may**, **could**, **would**. Then ask a classmate to classify these sentences into ability, permission, possibility, request, offer or invitation.

   1. _____

   _____

   2. _____

   _____

   3. _____

   _____

   4. _____

   _____

7 Look at the comic strip in activity 8 and answer. Then compare your answers with a classmate.

    a. Do you usually read comic strips? Which one is your favorite?

    _____

    b. Do you know any of the characters from this comic strip? What are their names?

    _____

    c. Look briefly at the comic strip, without reading it, and answer: what do you think it is about? Then read it and check if you were right.

    _____

    _____

8 Now, read the comic strip again and answer the following questions.

Peanuts, Charles Schulz © 1985 Peanuts Worldwide LLC./Dist. by Andrews McMeel Syndication

    a. What meal is Charlie Brown bringing Snoopy? What word from the text confirms that?

    _____

    b. What is Charlie Brown's intention in asking "It looks pretty good, doesn't it?"?

    _____

    c. Does Snoopy agree with Charlie Brown's opinion about the food?

    _____

    d. What does Snoopy really think of the food?

    _____

9 It's possible to say that in "Looks pretty good, doesn't it?" there is the following sentence structure:

    a. ◯ Positive sentence + negative tag question

    b. ◯ Negative sentence + positive tag question

10 If Snoopy added a tag question in his answer to Charlie Brown, how would the sentence be?

_____

11 Read and complete the gaps. Then match the sentences to the tag questions.

Tag Questions
I am late, **aren't I**?
We will go to the motocross exhibition, **won't we**?
She loves windsurfing, _____ **she**?
You _____ surf, **can't you**?
You _____ help me with this surfboard, **couldn't you**?
He _____ win the kayaking contest, **can he**?
They didn't buy the tickets for the game, _____ **they**?
She _____ like rock climbing, **does she**?
He won't go to the beach, **will he**?

a. You won't go rappelling,   ◯ doesn't he?

b. Peter wasn't at home yesterday,   ◯ did they?

c. My sister will go to the art exhibition,   ◯ was he?

d. The boys are going to school,   ◯ can't you?

e. You can go waterskiing,   ◯ won't she?

f. John rides his bicycle every Saturday,   ◯ aren't they?

g. The Browns didn't move to Texas,   ◯ will you?

12 Create sentences according to the tag questions given. Follow the example.

a. They were practicing rappel, weren't they?

b. _____, aren't I?

c. _____, don't you?

d. _____, was she?

e. _____, does it?

f. _____, couldn't you?

GRAMMAR HELPER

Go to page 170.

g. _____, didn't we?

LISTEN AND SPEAK

1 You are going to listen to an advertisement of Xtreme Adventure Camp. Based on what you know about summer or adventure camps and advertisements, answer these questions in pairs.

   a. Who usually goes to summer or adventure camps?

   b. What activities would you expect to find in adventure camps?

   c. What's the main objective of an advertisement? What pieces of information do you expect to hear in this audio?

2 Listen and check the option that indicates who speaks in the audio.

13

   a. ◯ Monitors and parents of children who went to the camp.

   b. ◯ Children and teens who want to visit the camp.

   c. ◯ Camp monitors and teens who usually go to the camp.

3 Listen to the first part of the audio and answer these questions. Then compare your
14 answers with a classmate.

   a. How long does Xtreme Adventure Camp provide its services? _____

   b. How many teens visited the camp during this time? _____

   c. Where are these teens usually from? _____

4 Listen again and check the activities offered by the camp.

15

a.

kayaking

b.

raft building

c.

river crossing

d.

waterskiing

5 Listen to the second part of the audio and complete the items with the correct
16 information.

a. Time of the year the camp is open: _____

b. How long you can stay in the camp: _____

c. Girl's nationality: _____

d. Nationality of the people she met at the camp: _____

e. The most important thing for the people working there: _____

f. What you have to do to get more information about the camp: _____

6 In pairs, talk about the advertisement and share your opinion about the camp and its
activities. Here you find some suggestions, but you may include other topics for discussion.

• advertisement/persuasive

• you/want to visit the camp

• activities you like and dislike

• activities you would include or exclude

• other: _____

PRONUNCIATION CORNER

1 Listen and act out the jazz chant.
17

I don't like a bit this old beat.

I don't like to sit on this old seat.

I don't like to eat a bit of this leek.

I think like a teen, that's what
I mean.

I don't like to drink hot tea,

I don't like the bzzzz of bees.

I don't like to feel pain in my knees.

I'd like to be like a teen, that's what
I mean.

2 Listen and practice the words.
18

| bit – beat   sick – seek   fit – feet   sit – seat   slip – sleep   fill – feel |

3 Match the pairs. Choose some of the words from the box.

| heat   deep   peace   leap   peek   sheep   keep   seen   feet   beat   seek   dip |

a. kip: _____

b. lip: _____

c. ship: _____

d. fit: _____

e. dip: _____

f. hit: _____

READ AND WRITE

1 Read the title and look at the pictures below. What is the text about?

◯ Team sports.   ◯ Exciting and dangerous sports.

2 Read the excerpt of the article below and answer the following questions in your notebook.

---

www.lonelyplanet.com/travel-tips-and-articles/20-unmissable-extreme-sports-and-where-to-try-them/40625

20 unmissable extreme sports (and where to try them)

Ready to feel your pulse racing? From zorbing to volcano boarding, we've rounded up 20 adrenaline-packed but accessible activities to tick off your bucket list – and the most stunning destinations to try them in.

Volcano boarding

The gist: pioneered by an Australian traveller in León, Nicaragua, volcano boarding is the art of zooming down the face of an active volcano on a reinforced plywood toboggan. Using your heels to brake and steer, it's possible to clock speeds of up to 90km/h. That's after you've hiked up the volcano, of course.

PixieMe/Shutterstock

Downhill mountain biking

Giles Clarke/Getty Images

The gist: using full-suspension bikes designed to float over rocks and tree roots, 'DH' bikers race down steep inclines peppered with obstacles.

Where to try it: DH biking Bolivia's so-called Death Road is one of the nation's most popular backpacker activities. Somewhat safer is Whistler Bike Park (bike.whistlerblackcomb.com) in Canada, at which winter ski runs morph into summer biking tracks.

Freshwater cave diving

The gist: ocean scuba is extreme enough for some, but descending into a hole in the earth to explore a submerged cave system is next-level stuff. Stalactites are usually the big draw.

Where to try it: Mexico's Yucatán Peninsula has the world's largest concentration of cenotes (sinkholes). Fringed by lush jungle, its crystal-clear turquoise pools are idyllic.

Don Couch/Barcroft Media/Getty Images

Heli-skiing or boarding

The gist: using a whirlybird to access untouched terrain, heli-skiing is quite technical, and you'll get more bang (or in this case, powder) for your buck if you're an advanced skier or snowboarder.

Where to try it: widely banned in Europe, heli-skiing is popular in North America and New Zealand. Alaska's Chugach Mountains boast some of the world's deepest, softest powder.

[...]

Leo Mason/Popperfoto/Getty Images

Canyoning

arenysam/Shutterstock

The gist: also known as canyoneering and river trekking, this sport encourages participants to use a variety of techniques including climbing and rappelling to traverse scenic canyons.

Where to try it: canyoning is traditionally performed on a mountain with flowing water – there are plenty in Germany, France, Ecuador, Colombia and Norway.

[...]

Available at: <www.lonelyplanet.com/travel-tips-and-articles/20-unmissable-extreme-sports-and-where-to-try-them/40625c8c-8a11-5710-a052-1479d277bd61>. Accessed on: Mar. 12, 2019.

a. How fast can a person go down the face of a volcano when practicing volcano boarding?

b. Which countries seem to be the best options when it comes to downhill mountain biking?

c. Why is exploring a submerged cave system a next-level stuff?

d. Which extreme sport gives the chance to jump from a helicopter?

e. What are the techniques you can use to practice canyoning?

f. Would you practice any of these extreme sports? Why (not)?

g. In your opinion, would life be boring if there was no adventure? Why?

3 The original article mentions 20 extreme sports. Check the ones that, in your opinion, are part of the article. Then discuss your answers with a classmate.

The World Traveller/Shutterstock

zorbing

Mauricio Graiki/Shutterstock

skydiving

DarioZg/Shutterstock

long jump

Text 2

4 Look at the three comic strips below and check what you can find in all of them.

- a. ◯ routine actions
- b. ◯ camping activities
- c. ◯ different weather conditions
- d. ◯ the name of Jon's pets

5 Read the comic strips and check what you can infer from them.

1.

2.

3.

- a. ◯ Jon, Odie and Garfield love camping.
- b. ◯ Jon is excited about camping.
- c. ◯ Odie is a lazy dog.
- d. ◯ Garfield prefers staying home instead of going camping.
- e. ◯ Garfield and Odie love rainy days.

6 Considering that the term "*Sahib*", used by some people in India, refers to a man in position of authority, what can you say about Garfield personality?

_____

_____

_____

7 Answer the questions below.

a. How many panels are there in each comic strip?

_____

b. Look at the third panel of the comic strips. What do they have in common?

_____

c. Which is predominant in comic strips: verbal or non-verbal texts?

_____

d. Why are Garfield's and Odie's speech bubbles different from Jon's?

_____

8 Let's create comic strips! In pairs, think of characters, and of short and funny stories you'd
179 like to illustrate. Then follow the steps below to create three different comic strips.

a. Reflect on the questions:
   • How many panels will you create for your comic strips?
   • What will the design of the speech bubbles be?
   • Will non-verbal texts be predominant in the comic strips?
   • Which panel will present humor?

b. Write a draft of your comic strips and produce all the drawings.

c. Show them to the teacher and ask for correction.

d. Write and draw the final versions.

e. Publish them in the school website or blog.

_____

_____

_____

_____

_____

_____

_____

TIPS FOR LIFE

Safety in extreme sports

1 Read the text about extreme sport safety and discuss the tips with a classmate.

https://www.defibshop.co.uk/blog/defibshop-news/extreme-safety-health-extreme-sport/

Extreme sports are fun to watch, and even more fun to take part in. But they also come with extra risks [...] the risk of serious injury is higher and those taking part must take extra care:

- Don't go out alone: Since the chance of injury in extreme sports is high, [...] it will be much easier to get help if there are people around you. [...]

- Bring the right equipment: Don't cut corners – Helmets, goggles, gloves and padding were all created for specific purposes [...]

- Know your limits: Watching extreme sports on TV and taking part in them yourself are two very different things. [...] You should refrain from attempting them without proper coaching and practice. [...]

- Watch the weather: Make sure you always check weather reports before you set out, and avoid heading out if the weather looks bad.

Available at: <https://www.defibshop.co.uk/blog/defibshop-news/extreme-safety-health-extreme-sport/>.
Accessed on: Mar. 18, 2019.

2 What to do in an emergency situation? Check the appropriate sentences.

a. ◯ Make sure you are out of danger.

b. ◯ Walk to the closest shelter.

c. ◯ Call the emergency service (in Brasil, 192 for an ambulance or 193 for the firefighters).

d. ◯ If there's a victim, check his or her responses.

3 In groups, make a poster about safety in extreme sports. Then present it to the class.

CHECK YOUR PROGRESS	😃	😐	🙁
Extreme sports			
Modal Verbs (can/could/ may/might/would)			
Tag Questions			
Listening			
Speaking			
Reading			
Writing			

1 Complete the gaps with the correct verb form.

a. John _____ to the hospital last night because he _____ a cold. (go/have)

b. My mother _____ the piano right now. (play)

c. We _____ to a new and bigger house next year. (move)

d. Julia _____ in her bedroom when her father _____ home. (be/arrive)

e. My sister _____ a new dress because she _____ the school dance next week. (buy/go)

f. My brother _____ his bedroom once a week. (clean)

g. While I _____ my friend, my mother _____ me. (text/call)

2 Read the sentences and check the correct question tags.

a. Your grandparents live in Fortaleza, _____?

○ aren't they   ○ don't they

b. Your parents had dinner at the new Chinese restaurant downtown, _____?

○ weren't they   ○ didn't they

c. Thomas isn't from Canada, _____?

○ is he   ○ doesn't he

d. Paula can't swim very well, _____?

○ could she   ○ can she

e. Grandpa didn't buy a new car, _____?

○ did he   ○ doesn't he

f. Charlie, won't go to the concert, _____?

○ did he   ○ will he

3 Label the pictures. Then complete the sentences with your personal information.

a.
_____

c.
_____

e.
_____

b.
_____

d.
_____

f.
_____

a. My favorite extreme sport is _____.

b. I'd love to practice _____.

c. I'd never practice _____ because _____.

d. In my opinion, _____ is the most dangerous extreme sport.

e. I think _____ is the least dangerous extreme sport.

4 Fill in the gaps with the appropriate modal verbs.

a. Mom, I am not sure, but I think Emily _____ come home tomorrow. (possibility)

b. That Math problem was so difficult that even the teacher _____ solve it. (ability)

c. William, _____ you like some cake with your coffee? (offer)

d. Teacher, _____ I go to the nurse's office? My stomach hurts. (permission)

e. Hey, Daniel, _____ I use your cell phone to call my mom? Mine is dead. (permission)

f. Mr. Roberts, you _____ wait inside the office. (possibility/permission)

g. Bethany, _____ you like to go to the Lady Gaga's concert with me? (invitation)

h. Good morning, Ms. Davis! _____ you confirm that you received my e-mail? (request)

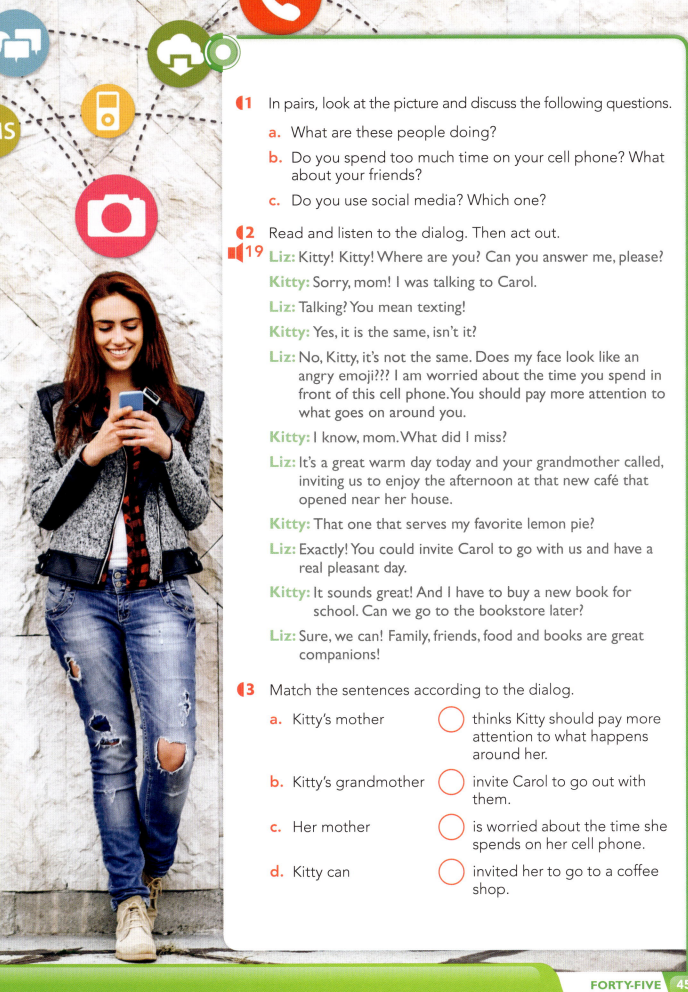

1 In pairs, look at the picture and discuss the following questions.

    a. What are these people doing?

    b. Do you spend too much time on your cell phone? What about your friends?

    c. Do you use social media? Which one?

2 Read and listen to the dialog. Then act out.

19

Liz: Kitty! Kitty! Where are you? Can you answer me, please?

Kitty: Sorry, mom! I was talking to Carol.

Liz: Talking? You mean texting!

Kitty: Yes, it is the same, isn't it?

Liz: No, Kitty, it's not the same. Does my face look like an angry emoji??? I am worried about the time you spend in front of this cell phone. You should pay more attention to what goes on around you.

Kitty: I know, mom. What did I miss?

Liz: It's a great warm day today and your grandmother called, inviting us to enjoy the afternoon at that new café that opened near her house.

Kitty: That one that serves my favorite lemon pie?

Liz: Exactly! You could invite Carol to go with us and have a real pleasant day.

Kitty: It sounds great! And I have to buy a new book for school. Can we go to the bookstore later?

Liz: Sure, we can! Family, friends, food and books are great companions!

3 Match the sentences according to the dialog.

    a. Kitty's mother   ◯   thinks Kitty should pay more attention to what happens around her.

    b. Kitty's grandmother   ◯   invite Carol to go out with them.

    c. Her mother   ◯   is worried about the time she spends on her cell phone.

    d. Kitty can   ◯   invited her to go to a coffee shop.

THINKING AHEAD

1 Are you an internet addict? Take the quiz and find out.

17:28   89%

a. When using the internet do you find that you lose track of time and feel surprised when you realize the time spent surfing the web?

○ Rarely   ○ Sometimes   ○ Often

b. Have you been ashamed of or tried to hide how much time you spend on your internet-connected device?

○ Rarely   ○ Sometimes   ○ Often

c. Do you find yourself wondering about things on the internet (chat, text messages, website updates) when you are not able to be online?

○ Rarely   ○ Sometimes   ○ Often

d. Are you trying to fall asleep while browsing the internet, but having trouble doing so?

○ Rarely   ○ Sometimes   ○ Often

e. Do you find yourself frustrated and/or upset when others seek your attention while you are online?

○ Rarely   ○ Sometimes   ○ Often

f. Have you experienced issues related to sore fingers/thumbs, eye strain, numbness of extremities, or other physical complications from long periods of internet use?

○ Rarely   ○ Sometimes   ○ Often

g. Has anyone in your personal life expressed concerns about the amount of time you spend on the internet?

○ Rarely   ○ Sometimes   ○ Often

h. Do you find yourself using the internet in specific situations where it might be less appropriate? For example, at school during class, while at work despite rules against it, during a ceremony (funeral/wedding/service), at a theater during a concert/play/movie, etc.

○ Rarely   ○ Sometimes   ○ Often

> **Score: Rarely** - 0 point/**Sometimes** - 1 point/**Often** - 2 points
> **Result: 16-12:** you are definitely tech addict.
>   **11-8:** you use tech a lot, but you are not an addict, it's OK!
>   **7-0:** you use common sense to deal with tech.

Available at: <https://www.psycom.net/internet-addiction-test-quiz>. Accessed on: Mar. 19, 2019.

Banco de imagens/Arquivo da editora

WORD WORK

1 Read and listen to what people can do online. Which activity is your favorite?

Send audio messages.

Watch TV series.

Make, edit and post videos.

Play interactive games.

Take and post selfies.

Watch clips and concerts.

Download apps.

Send text messages.

Chat with friends on social media.

Visit blogs and vlogs.

2 Read about other things you can do online and add two more items to the list. Then share them with your classmates.

- Research prices and products for online shopping.
- Watch movies, TV series, sports and documentaries.
- Share pictures and videos with friends and family.
- Virtually visit art museums around the world.
- Tour the Solar System.
- Check what is going on in the world.
- Read e-books and comic books.
- _____
- _____

3 In your opinion, what kind of devices teenagers would like to have? Why?

video game

smart TV

tablet

smartphone

4 Now think of two more devices teenagers would like to have and write down their names.

_____

_____

5 In pairs, go back to activity 1 and number them from 1 to 10 according to your preference. Being 10 the one you like the most and 1 the one you least like.

TIME FOR A GAME

Let's play **Scrambled Words** and **Communicative Game.**

FOCUS ON LANGUAGE

1 Read the comic strip and pay attention to the highlighted words. Then complete the chart with the missing words.

Subject Pronouns			he		it			they
Possessive Adjectives				her	its			their
Possessive Pronouns	mine		his	hers	–	ours		

2 Now read the sentences below, circle the Possessive Adjectives and underline the Possessive Pronouns.

a.

Whose smartphone is this?
This is my smartphone.
This smartphone is mine.

b.

Whose tablets are these?
These are their tablets.
These tablets are theirs.

c.

Whose laptop is this?
This is her laptop.
This laptop is hers.

3 Complete the sentences with Possessive Adjectives.

GRAMMAR HELPER

Go to page 170.

a. Do you think that most people like _____ devices?

b. I have a blog where I write _____ opinions about the books I read.

c. My sister and I have a new laptop where we keep _____ songs and photos.

d. I like to chat with Carol's friends on the internet. _____ friends are cool.

4 Read the sign and the cartoon paying special attention to the highlighted words. Then complete the sentence with **should** or **must**.

Banco de imagens/Arquivo da editora

© Dave Coverly/Dave Coverly and the Cartoonist Group.

MAYBE WE SHOULD PUT AWAY OUR PHONES – SHE'S TRYING TO TEXT ON A CRACKER.

NOTICE

STUDENTS MUST TURN OFF CELLULAR PHONES BEFORE ENTERING SCHOOL BUILDING

We use _____ to talk about a strong obligation and

_____ to talk about a moral obligation or advice.

5 Now read the chart and add your own examples.

Modal Verbs		
Should (advice/obligation)	**Must** (obligation)	**Mustn't** (prohibition)
_____	I **must** hurry. I'm late for school.	We **mustn't** throw garbage on the streets.
You **shouldn't** spend too much time on social media.	_____	She **mustn't** use the computer late at night. Her parents don't allow her to do so.
Should I see a doctor?	**Must** children have limited access to cell phones?	_____

LANGUAGE **TIPS**

Have to is used similarly to **must**, to talk about **obligations** in the affirmative form.
*You **have to** wear uniform for school.*
Don't have to expresses the idea of something that **is not necessary**.
*She **doesn't have to** take her phone everywhere.*

GRAMMAR **HELPER**

Go to page 171.

6 Write five questions using the modal verbs: **can**, **could**, **may**, **should**, **would**, and **have to**.

1. _____

2. _____

3. _____

4. _____

5. _____

7 Now, ask a classmate to answer the questions from activity 6. Register his/her answers and report to the other students and teacher. Change roles.

8 In pairs, read the following situations and write interrogative sentences using the modal verbs from the box.

| must | may | can | ~~could~~ | would | should |

a. You want to borrow your friend's tablet.

Could I borrow your tablet, please?

b. Your phone is broken. You need to call your father. You want to use your friend's phone.

c. Your teacher says it is an obligation to be at the computer room tomorrow at 8 o'clock.

d. You want to invite a friend to your house for a sleepover.

e. You are at the library. You want to use the computer to do some research.

f. Your friend has been bullied on the internet. He wants a piece of advise on whether he should talk to his parents or the teacher.

9 Match each problem with the appropriate piece of advice.

a. Mom refuses to pay my cell phone bill.

b. I don't like when people share my photos.

c. That website requires my personal information.

d. I can't see very well with these glasses.

e. My grades are bad.

◯ You should never give out your personal information.

◯ You should see an eye doctor and stay away from screens for a while.

◯ You should study harder and stop playing online games all the time.

◯ You shouldn't post your photos on social media.

◯ You should talk less on the cell phone.

LISTEN AND SPEAK

◀1 You are going to listen to a PSA (public service announcement) about digital citizenship. The PSA is presented by Zach Marks, the creator of Grom Social, a safe social network for kids and teens. Based on what you already know about being a good digital citizen, write down five to eight words you expect to listen.

_____

◀2
21 Listen to the PSA and check two aspects that a good digital citizen needs to be cautious about.

a. ◯ advertisement
b. ◯ digital footprint
c. ◯ fake news

d. ◯ cyberbullying
e. ◯ hacking
f. ◯ digital piracy

◀3
22 Listen again, take notes and answer the following questions. In pairs, compare your answers.

a. What does digital footprint mean?

_____
_____

b. How long does a digital footprint last?

_____

c. What do some people use as a pretext to become bullies?

_____
_____

d. What can you do if your friends are cyberbullying someone?

_____
_____

◀4
23 At the end of the audio, Zach explains that a good way to remember this information when posting online is to use the acronym THINK. What does each letter mean?

T – _____

H – _____

I – _____

N – _____

K – _____

5 In the PSA, Zach asks the following questions directly to the audience. Discuss them with your teacher and classmates.

   a. Considering the digital footprint, how do you want to represent yourself online?

   b. How would you feel if you were being bullied or threatened online?

6 In groups of four, go back to the list in activity 2 and prepare an oral presentation about the proposed items. Follow the steps below.

   a. Do some research and write about each item.

   b. Include other items to the list, too.

   c. You can learn more about the subject on: <https://www.kiddle.co/> and <https://duckduckgo.com>. Accessed on: Mar. 21, 2019.

   d. Watch this video for further information and take notes: <https://www.youtube.com/watch?v=gYe11RNGtZU>. Accessed on: Mar. 21, 2019.

   e. Present your findings to your classmates and teacher.

PRONUNCIATION CORNER

1 Listen and act out the jazz chant.
🔊**24**

   A: If you are bad you should stay in bed.

   B: Are you mad? I don't understand…

   A: You don't know where it is your handbag!!!

   A: The handbag is in your hand!

   B: In my hand? My handbag?

   A: Yes! Your handbag is in your left hand!

   A: Oh, Anne, I don't understand…

   B: Oh, Allan sorry…, I'm not mad!!!

2 Listen and practice the sounds below.
🔊**25**

man – men	said – sad	pen – pan
bed – bad	x – axe	

3 Now, in pairs, give examples of words with similar sounds.

LANGUAGE TIPS

The pairs of words, as *pin* and *bin*, or *bet* and *bad*, differing only by one sound in the same position in each word, are called **minimal pairs**.

READ AND WRITE

Text 1

1 In pairs, discuss the questions below and take notes. Then share your ideas with your classmates.

   a. What role does technology play in your social and school life? Give some examples.

   b. Do you have enough digital literacy skills to achieve your goals or do you need to learn new ones? Justify your answer.

2 Read the article below and check the correct alternatives to complete the sentences.

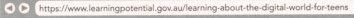

https://www.learningpotential.gov.au/learning-about-the-digital-world-for-teens

Wanted: digital literacy skills

Technology is constantly developing and changing the way we live and work. As the world continues to become more digitized and automated, digital literacy skills are going to become more and more important. But what is digital literacy and what can you do to support your teen to develop their digital literacy skills?

What is digital literacy?

Digital literacy is the knowledge and ability to use technology critically and creatively to find information, solve problems or complete tasks. It is also about knowing how to act safely and respectfully online.

Even though teenagers today are 'digital natives' (they were born into a technological world), digital literacy doesn't necessarily come naturally to them. Teens may find it easy to locate information online, but **do they have the skills to examine it critically, to know whether it is trustworthy and accurate? They may regularly see ads on TV, but are they aware that advertising is intended to manipulate the audience into buying a product? They may be able to shoot off a quick text message, but do they know the conventions of other online** forms of **communication? They may easily upload photos to social media sites, but do they know how to act responsibly and safely while online? What is happening in schools?**

arek_malang/Shutterstock

Digital literacy is already a focus in schools. Digital Technologies have been developed as one of the learning areas of the Australian Curriculum, and digital literacy skills are taught in English, alongside other, more traditional forms of literacy. Schools are recognising that digital technologies impact all areas of our lives and are using technology across all subject areas in new ways. Students are able to use a wide range of technologies to gather information, solve problems, be creative and collaborate with their peers, while also thinking critically. [...]

Available at: <https://www.learningpotential.gov.au/learning-about-the-digital-world-for-teens>. Accessed on: Mar. 19, 2019.

a. The target audience of this article is mainly...

   ◯ teachers and school staff.   ◯ parents or guardians.

b. The fragment which proves the previous answer is...

   ◯ "Schools are recognising that digital technologies impact all areas of our lives and are using technology across all subject areas in new ways".

   ◯ "But what is digital literacy and what can you do to support your teen to develop their digital literacy skills?"

3 Read the excerpts of the article and write **O** (opinion) or **F** (fact).

a. ◯ "Teens may find it easy to locate information online [...]"

b. ◯ "Digital literacy is the knowledge and ability to use technology critically and creatively to find information, solve problems or complete tasks. [...]"

c. ◯ "Digital Technologies have been developed as one of the learning areas of the Australian Curriculum [...]"

d. ◯ "Students are able to use a wide range of problems, be creative and collaborate with their peers [...]"

4 Go back to the text in activity 2 and read the highlighted fragment. Then reflect on the questions below.

a. Do you believe these questions are in your parents' or guardians' mind? Why (not)?

_____

_____

b. If these questions were asked to your parents or guardians, what would be the answers?

_____

_____

c. Do you consider yourself digitally literate? Why (not)?

_____

_____

d. List some examples of activities that are typical of someone who is digitally literate.

_____

_____

e. Give some examples of attitudes that, in your opinion, help to promote digital literacy.

_____

_____

Text 2

5 Answer the questions below in your notebook. Then compare your answers with your classmates'.

a. How many hours do you spend on the internet every day?

b. Is the number of hours you, your friends and classmates spend online the same? What can you infer about it?

6 Read the text and the graphs attentivelly. Then underline the wrong information in the following sentences and correct them.

Teens, Social Media & Technology 2018

YouTube, Instagram and Snapchat are the most popular online platforms among teens. Fully 95% of teens have access to a smartphone, and 45% say they are online 'almost constantly'

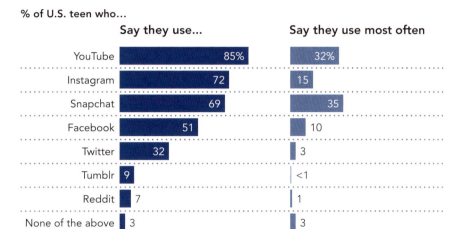

% of U.S. teen who…

Say they use… | **Say they use most often**

	Say they use…	Say they use most often
YouTube	85%	32%
Instagram	72	15
Snapchat	69	35
Facebook	51	10
Twitter	32	3
Tumblr	9	<1
Reddit	7	1
None of the above	3	3

Note: Figures in first column add to more than 100% because multiple responses were allowed. Question about most-used site was asked only of respondents who use multiple sites; results have been recalculated to include those who use only one site. Respondents who did not give an answer are not shown.

Source: Survey conducted March 7–April 10, 2018.

"Teens, Social Media & Technology 2018"

Pew Research Center

Teens have mixed views on the impact of social media on their lives

Teens have mixed views on social media's effect on people their age; many say it helps them connect with others, some express concerns about bullying

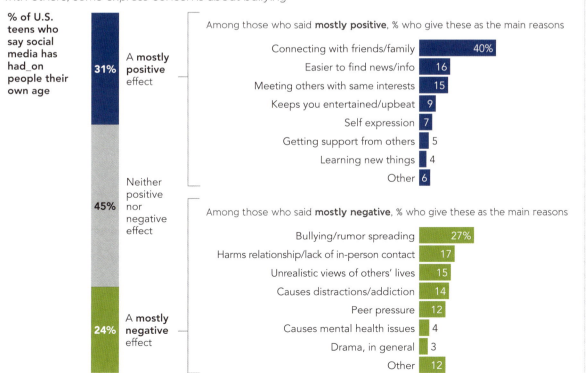

% of U.S. teens who say social media has had_on people their own age

31%	A **mostly positive** effect
45%	Neither positive nor negative effect
24%	A **mostly negative** effect

Among those who said **mostly positive**, % who give these as the main reasons

Connecting with friends/family	40%
Easier to find news/info	16
Meeting others with same interests	15
Keeps you entertained/upbeat	9
Self expression	7
Getting support from others	5
Learning new things	4
Other	6

Among those who said **mostly negative**, % who give these as the main reasons

Bullying/rumor spreading	27%
Harms relationship/lack of in-person contact	17
Unrealistic views of others' lives	15
Causes distractions/addiction	14
Peer pressure	12
Causes mental health issues	4
Drama, in general	3
Other	12

a. Most teens have access to smartphones and more than half of them are online constantly.

_____

b. Instagram is the most popular online platform among American teens.

_____

c. Tumblr is not as popular as Facebook, but 32% of teens prefer to access this platform.

_____

d. When it comes to percentage, the difference between Snapchat and Twitter is 51%.

_____

7 The two graphs represent the social media preferences of American teenagers. What about the preferences of Brazilian teenagers? Let's do some research and find out!

181

a. In pairs, create some questions about Brazilian teenagers' social media preferences and how it impacts their lives. Are their views negative, positive or neutral?

b. Do not forget to ask them why.

c. Show the questions to the teacher and do all the necessary adjustments.

d. Collect the data, analyze it, and create a graph.

e. Show the draft to your Math teacher so that he/she can check if the percentages are correct.

f. Produce a final version of the graph and a small paragraph introducing it. Then publish it in the school website or blog.

_____
_____
_____
_____
_____
_____
_____
_____
_____
_____

TIPS FOR LIFE

Internet safety

1 In pairs, match the columns in order to form tips to help you learn how to stay safe online and stand up for yourself, virtually or in person.

a. Save the evidence.

b. Google yourself.

c. Think before you post.

d. Use memes for good, not evil.

e. Don't let rumors run rampant.

○ If you see people post or share false and hurtful rumors online, don't stand by – speak up.

○ Protect your online reputation by keeping track of what's out there. Embarrassing photos? Damaging posts? Find out how to remove them.

○ If you're being cyberbullied, keep a record. Take screenshots, save texts, and print posts.

○ Before you tweet, text, or tag, think twice.

○ Start a trend! Harness the humorous power of memes to spread kindness, not cruelty.

2 Do some research on different cyber security tips from activity 1. Then write two of your own tips, too. Share your tips with your classmates and teacher.

_____

_____

_____

_____

_____

CHECK YOUR PROGRESS	😃	😐	🙁
Things teenagers like to do online			
Modal Verbs (must/ should)			
Listening			
Speaking			
Reading			
Writing			

1 Look at the picture and discuss with your classmates.

    a. Do you exercise regularly or are you sedentary?

    b. For you, what can make a fitness routine easier?

2 Read and listen to the dialog. Then act out.

26

Kitty: I used to exercise a lot, but now I stopped, and I feel like such a couch potato. And you? How is your fitness program going?

Carol: Good! I have a workout routine: twice a week, I go to the gym. First, I do a warm-up, then I go cycling or jogging. After that, I do 10 to 15 sit-ups and finally 25 jumping jacks.

Kitty: It doesn't seem hard to do!

Carol: Actually, it isn't. I don't like the jumping jacks. But Edward, the guy who is my fitness trainer, said they are good for flexibility.

Kitty: How long does each segment take?

Carol: Only about 20 minutes.

Kitty: Great! I'm going to do it.

Carol: Working out gives you more energy. But first you must consult a certified trainer to create a fitness program that is good for you.

Kitty: For sure.

Carol: Well, what about a 30-minute walk?

Kitty: Alright! Let's go!

3 Check **T** (true) or **F** (false), according to the dialog.

    a. ◯ Carol exercises for about 20 minutes every day.

    b. ◯ Kitty is feeling like a couch potato because she exercises a lot.

    c. ◯ As Carol's trainer, Edward is responsible for her fitness program.

    d. ◯ Before starting a fitness program, it's important to see a professional.

1 Look at the poster below. It is about...

a. ◯ dancing.

b. ◯ exercising.

c. ◯ a costume party.

2 Read the poster and answer the questions. Then compare your answers in pairs.

a. Why did humans exercise a lot in the past?

_____

_____

b. Why are our lives easy nowadays?

_____

_____

c. How often do we have to exercise?

_____

_____

d. How many hours of sleep does a 11-year-old child need?

_____

_____

3 Read the poster again and check the item that represents a benefit of exercising.

a. ◯ The performance at studies gets better.

b. ◯ The brain gets very stimulated and it never rests.

c. ◯ The tiredness increases and it's possible to sleep anywhere.

4 Do you know other benefits of exercising? Discuss in small groups and share your ideas with your teacher and classmates.

A WORD WORK

1 Listen and say. Then write **A** (activity) or **E** (equipment).

27

cycling

exercise bike

power walking

stretching

jumping rope

sit-ups

barbell

treadmill

jogging

push-ups

jumping jacks

dumbbell weights

2 Read and match.

a. Lay down on your stomach. Put your hands on the floor. After that, raise your shoulders pressing against the floor with your hands.

b. Ride a bike at a constant speed. You can do it for 1 hour. It's a good exercise for your legs.

c. Lay down on your back and flex your legs. Raise your trunk and lay down again.

d. First, stand up. Then, pull your arms and your legs as much as you can.

e. Stand up and keep your legs together. Next, jump and open your legs at the same time as you raise your arms.

f. Jump over a rope so that it passes under your feet and over your head.

g. Run at a slow or leisurely pace.

h. Walk fast with good posture, always looking forward. Keep your chest raised and shoulders relaxed.

○ stretching
○ jogging
○ power walking
○ sit-ups
○ cycling
○ push-ups
○ jumping rope
○ jumping jacks

Martin Novak/Moment RF/Getty Images

3 Complete the sentences with the words from the box.

| dumbbell weights barbell treadmill exercise bike |

a. A _____ is a piece of indoor fitness equipment used for running without moving anywhere.

b. A _____ is a long bar with weights on its ends to help weight lifters get a good grip.

c. _____ are short bars with a weight on each end that you lift up and down to strengthen your muscles.

d. An _____ is used as fitness equipment, not as transportation.

TIME FOR A GAME

Let's play **Bingo** and **Word list**.

FOCUS ON LANGUAGE

1 In pairs, look at the chart and match.

Relative clauses and relative pronouns

1. Who

A friend of mine rides a bike to school. She is very active.

- A friend of mine **who** rides a bike to school is very active.

2. Which

A healthy lifestyle combines some behaviors. You adopt these behaviors to improve your life quality.

- A healthy lifestyle combines some behaviors **which** you adopt to improve your life quality.

3. Whose

He is the fitness trainer. His mother is his client.

- He is the fitness trainer **whose** mother is his client.

a. We use the relative pronoun *who*   ◯ when we refer to things, ideas, animals.

b. We use the relative pronoun *which*   ◯ as the possessive form of *who*.

c. We use the relative pronoun *whose*   ◯ when we refer to people.

2 Complete the sentences using **which**, **who**, or **whose**.

a. Nathalie is the girl _____ cousin is my friend.

b. Do you know anybody _____ birthday is on January 1st?

c. Almost all kinds of activities _____ exercise the body are good.

3 Join the sentences using **which** or **who**.

a. The book is very good. She wrote the book.

_____

GRAMMAR HELPER

Go to page 172.

b. I talked to the woman. She was riding an exercise bike.

_____

c. She is wearing new tennis shoes. They cost US$ 100.

_____

LANGUAGE TIPS

In informal situations, the relative pronoun **that** can be used in place of **who** (referring to people) and **which** (referring to things, ideas, animals):
A friend of mine **that/who** rides a bike to school is very active.
A healthy lifestyle combines behaviors **that/which** you adopt to improve your life quality.

4 Find classmates who... Write their names.

	Find in the class...	Name
a.	a girl who likes jumping ropes.	
b.	a boy who likes to eat vegetables.	
c.	someone who doesn't like working out.	
d.	someone whose father or mother exercises a lot.	

5 Read the sentence below, paying special attention to the words in bold. Then check the best option.

> **Carol**: [...] **First**, I do a warm up, **then** I go cycling or jogging. **After that**, I do 10 to 15 sit-ups and **finally** 25 jumping jacks.

The words in bold are used to show the...

a. ◯ reasons for Carol having a workout routine.

b. ◯ sequence in which Carol does the exercises.

c. ◯ frequency in which Carol goes to the gym.

6 Read Maria's to-do list for the afternoon and describe it using the words in bold from activity 5.

2:30 pm – volleyball

4:00 pm – swimming

5:00 pm – yoga

6:30 pm – meditation

Banco de imagens/Arquivo da editora

7 Think about things you usually do in a specific day of the week and, in your notebook, create a to-do list similar to Maria's. Then, in pairs, describe the sequence of your activities.

8 Read the cartoon, paying special attention to the highlighted words. Then complete the chart.

© Dave Coverly/Dave Coverly and the Cartoonist Group

Subject Pronouns	_____	you	_____	_____	_____	_____	_____	they
Object Pronouns	me	_____	him	her	it	us	you	_____

9 Complete the sentences with Object Pronouns.

a. Where is Jim? I can't find _____.

b. The dog is hungry. Please, feed _____.

c. We're late. Can you give _____ a ride?

d. I don't know Ms. Jones. Do you know _____?

e. I have a lot of homework to do. Can you help _____?

10 Rewrite the sentences replacing the underlined words with Object Pronouns or Subject Pronouns.

a. <u>Daniel</u> is working with <u>his mother</u>.

_____

b. <u>My mother</u> always phones <u>my sister and me</u>.

_____

c. <u>The student</u> is doing <u>her homework</u> at school.

_____

11 Read the cartoon and check the correct option.

The construction **used to** describes something that happened...

a. ◯ regularly in the past.

b. ◯ just once in the past.

c. ◯ in the past and still happens in the present.

12 Look at the chart and add three more examples.

Used to
Affirmative: When I was child, I used to swim every day.
Interrogative: Did you use to do judo when you were young?
Negative: When I was living in Canada, I didn't use to exercise.

13 Look at the pictures. What do these people used to do?

a.

b.

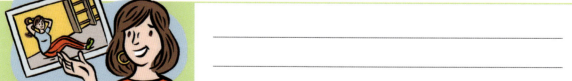

c.

LISTEN AND SPEAK

1 The following expressions were extracted from an informative video you are going to listen. Based on them, what do you think the audio is going to be about? Choose the best option.

happier and healthier

mentally alert

lower back pain

Oxford University

breathing exercises

health benefits

National Institute of Health

musculoskeletal issues

a. ◯ Problems caused by yoga.

b. ◯ Benefits of yoga.

c. ◯ Yoga breathing exercises.

2 Now, listen and check your answer in activity 1.

🔊28

3 Listen to the first part of the audio again and write **T** (true) or **F** (false). Then compare your
🔊29 answers in pairs.

a. ◯ Yoga can only improve mental health.

b. ◯ People who have backpain and asthma can benefit from yoga.

c. ◯ The benefits of yoga include less stress and lower blood pressure.

d. ◯ You must practice yoga at least three times a week to feel its benefits.

4 Listen to the second part of the audio and check the correct answers.

🔊30
a. How many types of yoga are there?

◯ There are many types.   ◯ There are two types.

b. What does pranayama mean?

◯ It means to focus on flexibility and insane positions.

◯ It means to focus on deep breathing and gentle stretching.

c. Who can practice pranayama?

◯ Anyone.   ◯ Only experts in yoga.

CROSS CULTURAL

Yoga is a group of physical and mental practices originated in ancient India. **Pranayama** is a word from Sanskrit, an ancient language of India, used to describe a breathing technique in yoga.

5 Have you ever tried to practice yoga? If so, how was it? If not, would you like to try it? Why (not)? Talk to your classmates and teacher.

6 Ask and answer about your habits related to physical activities. Write in your notebook.

    a. Create five questions related to physical activities.

    b. In pairs, answer your classmate's questions and ask yours – take notes of your classmate's answers, you will need them.

    c. Change partners to report your classmate's answers and listen to him/her.

TO LEARN MORE

> You can find more information about yoga and its benefits in the following link: <https://www.youtube.com/watch?v=CU3HuPNsyG4>. Accessed on: Mar. 14, 2019.

PRONUNCIATION CORNER

1 Listen to the jazz chant and act out.
31

    A: Good afternoon, Luke!

    B: Good afternoon, Sue! What's that on your shoe?

    A: There's gum on my shoe!!!

    B: Who threw gum on your shoe?

    A: Tell me, was it you, Duke?

    C: No, it was June.

    A: Who? June?

    C: It was June.

    D: It wasn't me. It was Duke.

    C: It was you! It was you!

    B: Stop, Duke. Don't be rude!

    C: Sorry!

2 Listen and practice the following words.
32

Listen and practice the /u:/ sound. Notice it's a long sound.		Listen and practice the /u/ sound. Notice it's a short sound.	
shoe	through	look	would
news	chew	put	wood
whose		could	good
who	do	should	pull

Text 1

1 In your opinion, are you a couch potato? Why (not)?

_____

_____

_____

2 Answer the quiz and check the result. According to it, is your answer in activity 1 correct? If not, do you agree with the result?

ARE YOU A COUCH POTATO?

Couch potato is a lazy person who does nothing but sits on the couch and watch television while eating junk food. Many people are couch potatoes. Are you? Take the quiz and find out.

1 What is a regular dinner for you?

   a. Fast food every day.

   b. Fast food on the weekends.

   c. A nice balanced meal.

siamionau pavel/Shutterstock

2 Are you involved in sports?

   a. I did when I was little, but not anymore.

   b. One or two sports.

   c. Sports are my life.

3 How often in a week do you have dessert?

   a. 4-7 days.

   b. 2-3 days.

   c. Never.

4 If you do have dessert, how much do you have?

   a. A scoop or two of ice cream/a few cookies/cake.

   b. Low fat jelly or something healthy for you.

   c. I don't have dessert.

stockcreations/Shutterstock

5 There's a marathon of your favorite TV show in the world and it's going to be 48 hours long. What do you do?

  a. I skip work/school and stay up all night to watch it.

  b. I watch it until I fall asleep after work/school both nights.

  c. I don't watch it.

Erhan Inga/Shutterstock

6 When you are hungry, do you get something fast to eat or take time to make a snack for yourself?

  a. Something fast.

  b. It varies.

  c. Make a low fat snack.

7 Do you eat popcorn/pizza/sandwiches/chocolate while watching TV?

  a. Yes, I do.

  b. Sometimes.

  c. No, I don't.

JuliePhotos/Shutterstock

8 Do you like reading?

  a. No, I hate reading.

  b. Only gossip and sports magazines.

  c. Yes, I love books.

If the majority of your answers are letter **C**:	If the majority of your answers are letter **B**:	If the majority of your answers are letter **A**:
Congratulations to you! You are definitely not a couch potato. You know what healthy food is. TV is really not your priority in life! Keep TV watching to a minimum and enjoy life! That is the way to go!	You are normally active. You know when to get off the couch, turn off the TV and face the world. You're lucky you're not a big couch potato.	You are definitely a couch potato! You need to learn how to turn off your TV and stop sitting on your couch. No more cupcakes, potato chips or soda all night. No more being a couch potato!

Based on: <https://www.gotoquiz.com/are_you_a_couch_potato>. Accessed on: Mar. 13, 2019.

❸ Imagine you are surfing on the internet and find this quiz. Would you like to answer it? Why (not)?

_____

_____

_____

Text 2

4 Look at the text below. It's a

a. ⭕ flyer about a yoga class.

c. ⭕ poster about the benefits of yoga.

b. ⭕ cartoon about yoga fans.

5 Read the flyer below and answer the questions.

Filipe Rocha/Arquivo da editora

hope

mental clarity

breath

you

peace

balance

strength

Yoga for Everybody

in Rainbow View, with Olivia Poe

When: Tuesday & Thursday
Time: 6:00-7:30 pm
Beginning: June 8th, 2019

Where: Rainbow View, Ocean Street
Class card special: 4 classes for $44
Drop in: $14

For more information:

www.rainbowview.com
rainbowview@mail.com
707.308.4567

Private classes available & baby boot camp yoga

fizkes/Shutterstock

Olivia's intention is to help people enjoying moving and being in their body. Every-body can do yoga, at every phase of life, age, and ability.

a. What's the instructor's intention?

_____

b. Who can do yoga?

_____

c. What are the benefits of yoga?

_____

6 Check what we can find in the flyer.

a. ◯ Personal information about the instructor.

b. ◯ Pictures and concise text in order to grab people's attention.

c. ◯ Information about prices.

d. ◯ Information about date and place.

e. ◯ Contact information: e-mail, phone number and website.

f. ◯ Social Media information.

7 What is the objective of the flyer?

_____

_____

8 What is the target audience of this flyer?

_____

_____

9 The flyer brings a wordplay "Every-Body". What is the meaning of it? Talk to a classmate and answer the question.

_____

_____

_____

10 Read the following sentences and choose the one that describes a flyer properly.

a. ◯ Flyers announce a product, service or event in a simple way. They usually combine verbal and non-verbal information (text and images) to inform their audience.

b. ◯ Flyers contain fictional data and present information as a long story that contains images and text. They are a form of literary text.

11 A scavenger hunt will take place in your school. In pairs, create a flyer to advertise the

183 event. Follow the steps below.

a. In your notebook, write down all the necessary information.

b. Also, create a compelling sentence for the top of the flyer.

c. Show these drafts to the teacher.

d. Do all the adjustments, rewriting the text in a sheet of paper.

e. Choose color and pictures to grab readers' attention.

f. Produce the final version.

TIPS FOR LIFE

Physical and mental safety

1 In pairs, look at the poster and answer the questions. Then discuss them with your classmate.

   a. In your opinion, what does the picture in the poster represent?

   _____

   _____

   b. Do you agree with the sentence: "Health and Physical Education promotes a physically and emotionally safe learning environment"? Why (not)?

   _____

   _____

   _____

   c. In your opinion, which T-shirt message is the most important? Why?

   _____

   _____

2 In pairs, make a poster writing the sentence *I learn best because...* and completing it with your own ideas.

Divulgação/Reprinted with permission from Ophea - All About H&PE: Physical and Emotional Safety Poster, 2016.

CHECK YOUR PROGRESS

	😃	😐	🙁
Keeping fit			
Relative Pronouns/ Adverbs of sequence/ Object Pronouns/Used to			
Listening			
Speaking			
Reading			
Writing			

1 Rewrite the sentences replacing the words in bold by their corresponding possessives.

a. **Kitty and Carol's** gym special sneakers aren't here.

_____

b. **The athletes'** gym jackets and pants are new.

_____

c. These are **John's** dumbbell weights. I can't find **your dumbbell weights**, Kate.

_____

d. Who is wearing green track suits? My friends and **Carol's friends**.

_____

e. Miss Jones told her students to open **the English books**.

_____

2 Fill in the gaps with **must**, **mustn't**, **have to** or **should**.

a. My father _____ exercise more often to relieve his work stress.

b. Pay attention, Charlie! You _____ be at school at 8:00 o'clock sharp.

c. Do you _____ download this app right now?

d. You _____ read more books instead of using your cell phone all the time.

e. You _____ text your friends during classes.

3 Read and circle the correct Object Pronouns to complete the sentences below.

a. Jim has a new treadmill. He bought **it/them** yesterday.

b. Push-ups are very difficult for me. I can't do **them/him**.

c. I miss Natalie so much. I'm going to call **her/him** tonight.

d. I didn't invite Louis to my party. I don't like **him/us**, actually.

e. Chris and I are your friends, Kelly. You can go out with **them/us**.

4 Complete the sentences using **who**, **which** or **whose**.

a. The old man _____ lives next door goes cycling every morning.

b. That is the new state-of-the-art treadmill _____ I told you about.

c. Johnny is the guy _____ goes to the gym and works out twice a week.

d. I have a friend _____ cousin is a famous top model.

5 Complete the sentences with **used to** and the expressions from the box.

chat on the internet	play games alone	eat junk food	watch cartoons

a. I _____, but now I prefer playing interactive games with my friends.

b. My brother Tyler _____, but now he prefers going to the movies or dancing.

c. Sheila _____, but now she watches TV series.

d. Barbara _____, but now she only eats healthy and organic food.

6 Read the text about Billy's past and present habits. Then fill in the gaps using the verbs given.

Monkey Business Images/Shutterstock

Billy is in shape, but two years ago his life was different. He _____ (not exercise) – now he _____ (go) to the gym every day. Also, he _____ (eat) junk food every day – now he _____ (eat) fruit and vegetables. As a result, Billy _____ (sleep) like a baby – he _____ (not sleep) well in the past.

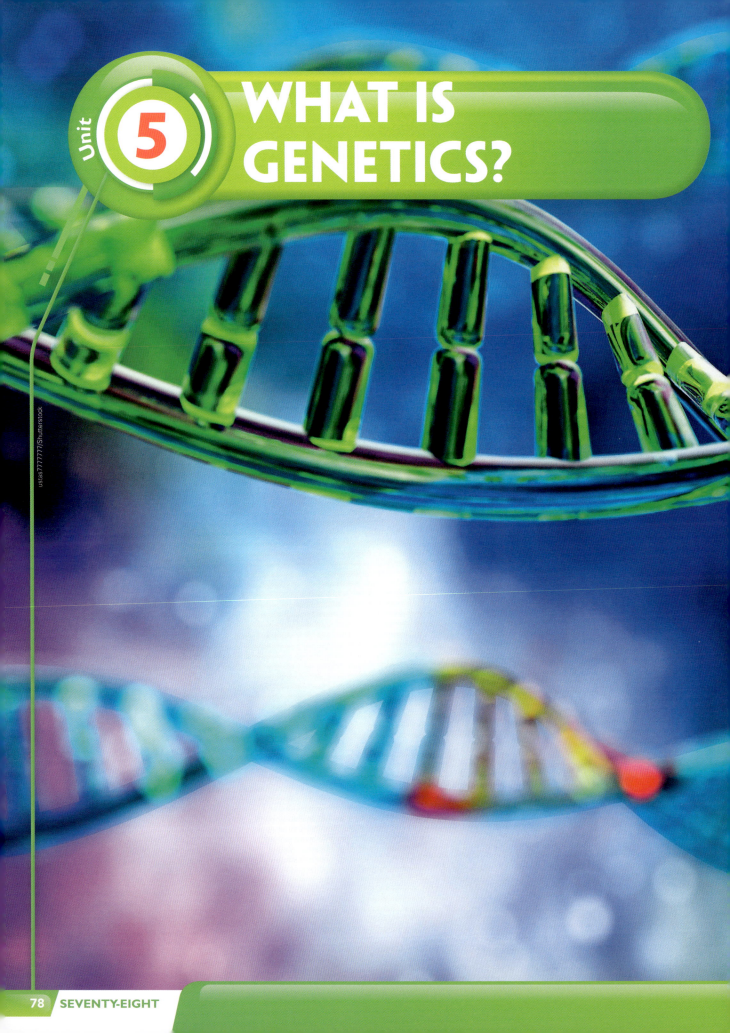

Unit 5
WHAT IS GENETICS?

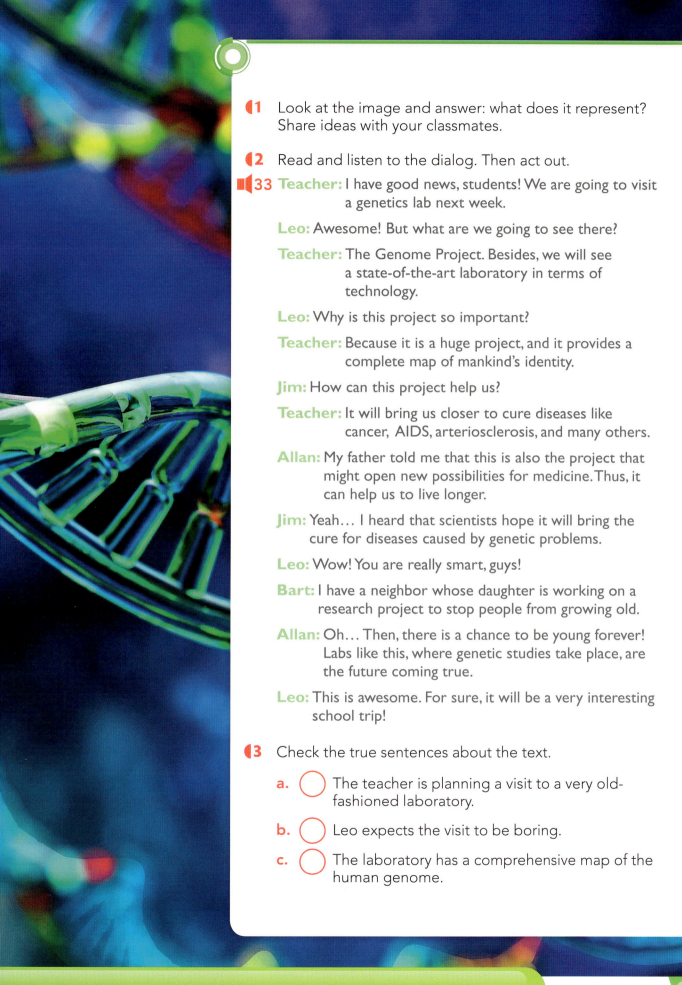

1 Look at the image and answer: what does it represent? Share ideas with your classmates.

2 Read and listen to the dialog. Then act out.

33 Teacher: I have good news, students! We are going to visit a genetics lab next week.

Leo: Awesome! But what are we going to see there?

Teacher: The Genome Project. Besides, we will see a state-of-the-art laboratory in terms of technology.

Leo: Why is this project so important?

Teacher: Because it is a huge project, and it provides a complete map of mankind's identity.

Jim: How can this project help us?

Teacher: It will bring us closer to cure diseases like cancer, AIDS, arteriosclerosis, and many others.

Allan: My father told me that this is also the project that might open new possibilities for medicine. Thus, it can help us to live longer.

Jim: Yeah… I heard that scientists hope it will bring the cure for diseases caused by genetic problems.

Leo: Wow! You are really smart, guys!

Bart: I have a neighbor whose daughter is working on a research project to stop people from growing old.

Allan: Oh… Then, there is a chance to be young forever! Labs like this, where genetic studies take place, are the future coming true.

Leo: This is awesome. For sure, it will be a very interesting school trip!

3 Check the true sentences about the text.

a. ◯ The teacher is planning a visit to a very old-fashioned laboratory.

b. ◯ Leo expects the visit to be boring.

c. ◯ The laboratory has a comprehensive map of the human genome.

THINKING AHEAD

1 Observe the fact sheet in activity 2 and answer: what is it about?

2 Now, read the following fact sheet attentively. In pairs, fill in the blanks with the correct topic below.

a. Choose the Best Medicine and Correct Dose

b. Screen Newborns for Certain Treatable Conditions

c. Diagnose Your Disease

d. Discover Genetic Factors that Increase Your Disease Risk

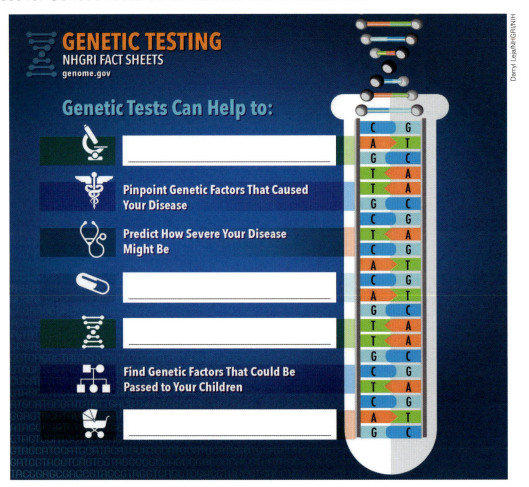

GENETIC TESTING
NHGRI FACT SHEETS
genome.gov

Darryl Leja/NHGRI/NIH

Genetic Tests Can Help to:

_____

Pinpoint Genetic Factors That Caused Your Disease

Predict How Severe Your Disease Might Be

_____

_____

Find Genetic Factors That Could Be Passed to Your Children

_____

Fact sheet:

A sheet of paper giving useful information about a particular issue, especially one distributed for publicity purposes.

Available at: <https://en.oxforddictionaries.com/definition/us/fact_sheet>. Accessed on: Mar. 15, 2019.

Condition is a word widely used to refer to a disease or health problem.

WORD WORK

1 Let's talk about genetics! Listen and repeat.

34

gene manipulation

genetics

DNA

clone

embryo

human genome

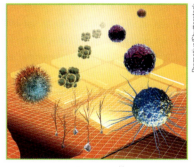

stem cell

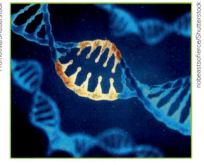

inherited disease

transgenic vegetable

chromosome

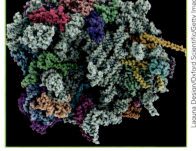

ribosome

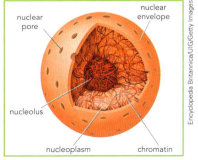

nuclear pore

nuclear envelope

nucleolus

nucleoplasm

chromatin

nucleus

2 Match the words and expressions to the definitions.

a. Embryo

b. Gene

c. DNA

d. Stem cell

e. Clone

f. Transgenic vegetable

g. Genome

( ) A cell or organism that is genetically identical to the unit or individual from which it was derived.

( ) A substance that carries genetic information in the cells of the body.

( ) A cell in a very early stage of development that can develop into any other type of cell.

( ) An animal or human in the early stages of development.

( ) All the genetic material of an organism.

( ) The basic physical unit of heredity.

( ) Any plant containing a gene or genes transferred from another species.

TO LEARN MORE

Gregor Mendel was an Austrian monk who discovered the basic principles of heredity through experiments in his garden. Mendel's observations became the foundation of modern genetics and the study of heredity, and he is widely considered a pioneer in the field of genetics.

Available at: <www.biography.com/people/gregor-mendel-39282>. Accessed on: Mar. 15, 2019.

TIME FOR A GAME

Let's play **Alphabet Game** and **Spelling Bee**!

3 Find eight words related to genetics in the word search below.

D	F	G	H	J	K	L	Q	D	S	X	Z	M
E	R	T	Y	U	I	O	H	I	O	P	G	H
C	H	R	O	M	O	S	O	M	E	H	G	R
S	D	H	G	T	T	K	A	N	G	E	N	I
T	R	H	N	S	G	E	N	I	C	X	J	B
E	G	A	Z	F	I	G	I	A	K	P	T	O
M	E	M	C	D	C	F	E	L	M	Ã	Q	S
C	N	H	D	B	L	O	E	N	B	O	M	O
E	E	D	N	A	A	I	R	I	O	F	R	M
L	T	H	P	V	N	U	I	G	W	M	X	E
L	I	A	C	N	E	E	A	S	Ç	B	E	H
D	C	S	N	U	C	L	E	U	S	P	G	V
F	S	H	A	S	D	X	C	B	N	M	P	Q

FOCUS ON LANGUAGE

1 Read the cartoon and discuss in pairs: is happiness an illusion? Is it a question for the brain or the heart?

2 In pairs, read the cartoon again and…

a. underline the correct options to complete the following sentence.
In the cartoon, the brain presents itself as **rational/emotional** while the heart is **logical/passional**.

b. choose the best meaning of **illusion** based on the context.

◯ a trick used for some magicians to cheat their audience.

◯ something that appears to exist but does not actually exist.

c. justify the use of the indefinite article **an** in "**an** illusion".

_____

3 Read the charts, add your own examples and compare them in pairs.

Indefinite articles (singular only)	
_a_ is used	**_an_ is used**
• before singular countable nouns (or adjectives) that begin with a consonant sound:	• before singular countable nouns (or adjectives) that begin with a vowel sound:
_____	_____

Don't use _a_ or _an_

• before plural nouns: **Genes** are part of DNA.
• before proper nouns (names of people and places): **Gregor Mendel**, Austrian botanist, is considered the "father of genetics".
• before uncountable nouns: Genes carry **information**.

LANGUAGE TIPS

Some vowels have a consonant sound. In these cases, we use the indefinite **a** before these nouns:
It's **a u**niversity.   Finland is **a E**uropean country.

When **h** is a silent letter, we use the article **an**:
I'll be back in **an h**our.   Louise is **an honor** student.

Definite article

the is used	*the* is not used
• in singular and plural sentences, referring to specific things and people, when the person knows what or who I am talking about: **The** man I talked about is here.	• with a noun used in general sense: Nature is perfect.
	• before proper names and possessives: My twin sister is not identical to me.
_____	_____

LANGUAGE TIPS

In general, the definite article (the) is not used before names of countries:

Brazil is a huge country.

But there are some exceptions, for example: **the** United States, **the** United Kingdom, **the** Netherlands.

◀4 Complete the fragment with the definite article **the** where necessary.

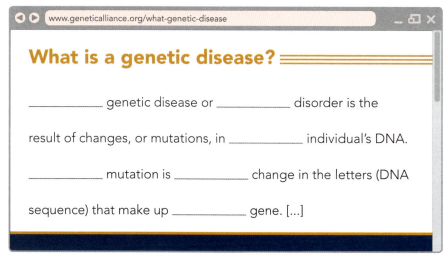

www.comicvine.com/x-gene-mutant/4015-40656/

X-Gene mutant characters

In *The Children of* _____ *Atom*, _____ mutants are individuals in _____ Marvel Universe who are born with an X-Gene that grants them superhuman abilities.

These mutants mark _____ next step in human evolution, known as *Homo* Superior. [...]

◀5 Complete the fragment with the indefinite article **a** or **an** if necessary.

www.geneticalliance.org/what-genetic-disease

What is a genetic disease?

_____ genetic disease or _____ disorder is the

result of changes, or mutations, in _____ individual's DNA.

_____ mutation is _____ change in the letters (DNA

sequence) that make up _____ gene. [...]

GRAMMAR HELPER

Go to page 174.

6 Read the text below paying close attention to the word in bold. Then check the appropriate answer.

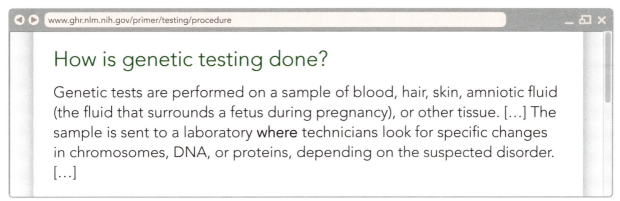

Available at: <https://ghr.nlm.nih.gov/primer/testing/procedure>. Accessed on: Mar. 2, 2019.

The pronoun **where** refers to...

a. ◯ places.

b. ◯ people.

c. ◯ things.

d. ◯ places and things.

e. ◯ places and people.

7 Complete the "**where**" sentences.

a. Near my house, there is a park where _____.

b. That's the supermarket where _____.

c. My uncle lives in a town where _____.

d. This genetic study will be held in a lab where _____.

8 Now, having in mind what you've learned so far about relative pronouns, match the columns.

Relative pronoun	Refers to
a. who	◯ animals and things
b. that	◯ people
c. which	◯ possession
d. whose	◯ places
e. where	◯ things, animals and people

GRAMMAR HELPER

Go to page 172.

9 Read the text and observe the words in bold. Complete the following sentences using them.

Why do my brother and I look so different?

There are two main reasons: The first is that the two of you didn't grow up the same way. **And** the second is that even though you have the same parents, you don't have the same genes. The way you grew up is what geneticists call your environment. It includes where you grow up, what you eat, and what you do. It **also** includes what your mom did and ate while she was pregnant with you. People are different in part **because** no two people grow up in the same environment. Not even twins are together all the time!

Available at: <https://genetics.thetech.org/ask/ask279>. Accessed on: Mar. 19, 2019.

a. _____ and _____ are used to connect two sentences, expressing the idea of **addition**.

b. _____ is used to connect two sentences, expressing the idea of **reason or cause**.

10 Fill in the blanks with the linking words from activity 9 and observe other linking words and their use.

Linking words	Idea	Examples
besides, _____, _____, as well as	addition	Geneticists work doing research **as well as** developing new genetic technologies.
consequently, thus, as a result, so	consequence	**Consequently/As a result**, scientists believe the future genetic testing will help many people.
but, however	contrast	I like studying Science, **but** genetics is very difficult.
in conclusion, summing up, finally	conclusion	**In conclusion/Summing up/Finally**, genetic testing will have an important impact in our future lives.
_____, as, since	giving reasons	**Since/As** you get one pair of chromosomes from your mother and one from your father, you get one gene from each one of them, too.
as long as, if	condition	You can go to the party **as long as/if** you study to your test.
first, then, secondly, before, after	time, sequence	Scientists researched animal's genome **before** studying human genome.
for sure, indeed, absolutely, clearly, undoubtedly	emphasis	Genetics advances are huge. **Undoubtedly**, this will be a new era.

11 Go back to the dialog on page 79 and find examples of linking words expressing ideas of: addition, contrast, reason, consequence, time and emphasis. Write them in your notebook.

LISTEN AND SPEAK

1 What do you know about longevity and life expectancy? In your notebook, list five words or expressions that come to your mind and share them with your classmates.

2 You are going to listen to two audios about longevity: part of a presentation given by a doctor and part of a news report. Listen and match the correct definition for presentation and for report.

35

a. Presentation

○ A talk giving information about something.

b. Report

○ The give a spoken or written account of something that one has observed, heard, done, or investigated.

3 Listen to the presentation and fill in the blanks.

36

to live longer	faster from illnesses	experience less aches and pains
we can enjoy life to the fullest		we won't be able

a. A benefit of being healthy: _____.

b. In bad health _____ to participate in many activities with our children, family and friends.

The advantages of people who are healthy:

c. They tend _____.

d. They _____.

e. They recover _____.

4 Listen to the news report and answer the questions.

37

a. Which countries are mentioned in the report? _____

b. Which country is famous for having the world's longest life expectancy? _____

c. Which country is expected to have the world's longest life expectancy by 2040? _____

d. Why are people from this country expected to live longer?

○ Because of their eating habits.

○ Because of their technology.

5   How good are your habits? Talk to a classmate about your good habits and the areas you need to improve to live a long and happy life.

Good habits you cultivate	Areas you need to improve

PRONUNCIATION CORNER

1   Listen and act out the jazz chant.

38

A: Mom, why are you so sad?

B: Nobody loves me.   **B:** Oh, my dear son...

B: I'm so sad.   **B:** You are perfect!

B: My heart hurts.   **B:** You are lovely!

B: I'm so unhappy!   **B:** You are wonderful!

A: I don't understand, mom…   **A:** Thanks, mom!

A: I love you very much!   **A:** Please, be happy!

A: You are perfect!   **B:** Now, I'm happy!

A: You are lovely!   **B:** I love you, son!

2   Listen and practice the words.

39

> Love – Son
>
> Must – Much
>
> Fun – Couple
>
> Glove – Enough

READ AND WRITE

Text 1

1 Read the headline of the news report below. Based on it, what is the text about?

a. ◯ It's about Science.

b. ◯ It's about animal cruelty.

c. ◯ It's about hunger and poverty.

2 Read the news report and answer the questions that follow.

www.downtoearth.org.in/news/health/now-chickens-lay-eggs-with-anti-cancer-drugs-63007

Now, chickens lay eggs with anti-cancer drugs

Norrie Russel/University of Edinburgh

These chickens have a human gene that enables them to lay eggs containing useful drugs

We already knew about presence of genetically modified ingredients in our food and also that animals were being gene-edited feed, but now animals too are being altered for human benefit. Researchers have modified the gene of chickens so as to make them lay eggs that will have drugs to treat patients with cancer and arthritis, find researchers from the Roslin Institute at the University of Edinburgh in Scotland.

Lissa Herron of Roslin Technologies in Edinburgh says the chickens, which were experimented on, were not mistreated rather they were pampered. "We are excited to develop this technology to its full potential, not just for human therapeutics in the future but also in the fields of research and animal health," says Herron.

The study offers a cost-effective method to produce certain types of drugs. High quantities of proteins can be recovered from each egg using a simple purification system. [...]

Also, the Edinburgh researchers found that this method is expected to be 100 times cheaper than producing the drugs in factories and chickens are best suited to produce the drug. [...]

The researchers believe that it would take them decades to get regulatory approvals to ensure this drug reaches people. [...]

Available at: <www.downtoearth.org.in/news/health/now-chickens-lay-eggs-with-anti-cancer-drugs-63007>.
Accessed on: Apr. 18, 2019.

a. According to the news report, genetically modified chickens will be able to lay eggs that contain drugs for arthritis and cancer. What is this statement based on?

_____

b. Considering the cost to produce drugs, what is the advantage of the method with genetically modified chickens?

_____

3 Which part of the news report proves that there is no cruelty against the chickens?

a. ◯ "Lissa Herron of Roslin Technologies in Edinburgh says the chickens, which were experimented on, were not mistreated rather they were pampered."

b. ◯ "The researchers believe that it would take them decades to get regulatory approvals to ensure this drug reaches people."

4. Why did the reporter reproduce the exact words of Dr Lissa Herron?

_____

Text 2

5 Look quickly at the cartoons in activity 2 and answer: where are the characters in the two situations?

_____

6 Now, read the cartoons. Check the sentences that are **not true** about them.

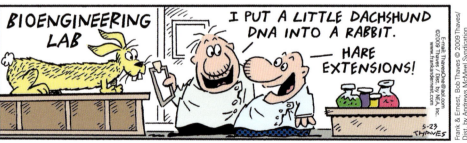

a. ◯ In both situations the scientists create a new animal.

b. ◯ In the second cartoon, the scientist used two animals to create a third one.

c. ◯ The scientists are not happy with the new inventions.

d. ◯ In both comics, the DNA was crucial to accomplish the scientific experiment.

7 Answer the questions below in your notebook.

    a. What makes the two labs different from each other?

    b. What do the cartoons and the text on page 89 have in common?

Text 3

8 You are going to read a text about genes and DNA. What kind of information do you expect to find? Share your ideas with your classmates.

9 Read the text and check true or false.

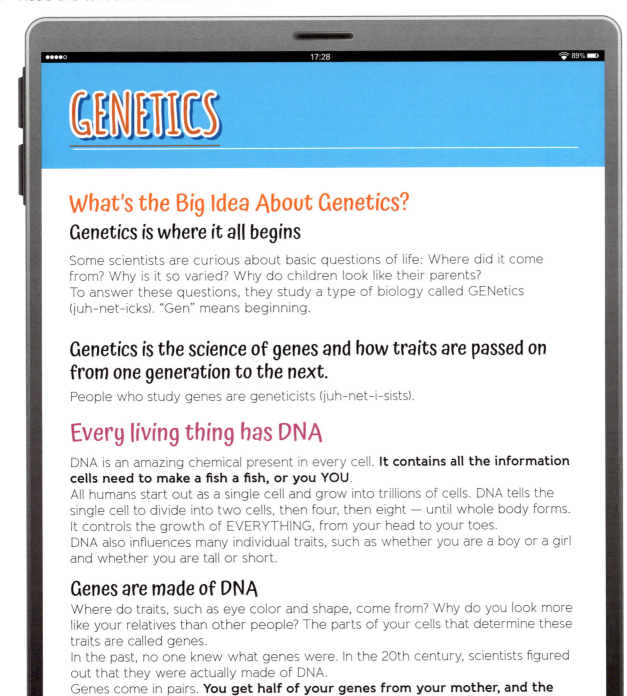

GENETICS

What's the Big Idea About Genetics?
Genetics is where it all begins

Some scientists are curious about basic questions of life: Where did it come from? Why is it so varied? Why do children look like their parents?
To answer these questions, they study a type of biology called GENetics (juh-net-icks). "Gen" means beginning.

Genetics is the science of genes and how traits are passed on from one generation to the next.

People who study genes are geneticists (juh-net-i-sists).

Every living thing has DNA

DNA is an amazing chemical present in every cell. **It contains all the information cells need to make a fish a fish, or you YOU.**
All humans start out as a single cell and grow into trillions of cells. DNA tells the single cell to divide into two cells, then four, then eight — until whole body forms.
It controls the growth of EVERYTHING, from your head to your toes.
DNA also influences many individual traits, such as whether you are a boy or a girl and whether you are tall or short.

Genes are made of DNA

Where do traits, such as eye color and shape, come from? Why do you look more like your relatives than other people? The parts of your cells that determine these traits are called genes.
In the past, no one knew what genes were. In the 20th century, scientists figured out that they were actually made of DNA.
Genes come in pairs. **You get half of your genes from your mother, and the other half from your father.**

We gather clues about life by studying genes

As we discover more about how genes work, we will be able to understand how cells build complex organisms — like humans.

Today, scientists are studying human genes to learn about traits and diseases. There are so many genes in humans — at least 30,000 of them — that it will take a long time to study everyone in detail and find out what it does.

A genome is all the DNA in a cell, including all the genes

Recently, new technology has enabled scientists to look closely at the entire human genome.

They have also been able to describe the whole genomes of other animals, including those of bacteria, worms, flies, and mice. The science of genomics asks questions about all of these genes at once. Scientists can also compare genomes of different animals and figure out how they are similar and different.

Available at: <https://www.amnh.org/explore/ology/genetics/what-s-the-big-idea-about-genetics2>.
Accessed on: May 7, 2019.

	True	False
a. Genetics is the science of genes. It explains how traits are passed through generations.		
b. All humans start out as a single small cell and grow into a single big one.		
c. You get most of your genes from your mother.		
d. Today, scientists are studying human genes to learn about traits and diseases.		
e. The genome of an organism is the whole of its hereditary information encoded in its DNA.		

10 What about testing your knowledge of Biology and Genetics? In pairs, create a
185 questionnaire with ten questions about different topics of Biology and Genetics. Follow the instructions.

- Do some research in your books. You can also use the text that you have just read.

- Write ten questions. The answers must be objective so you can correct them quickly.

- Show the questions you wrote to your teacher for language review.

- Show them to your Biology or Science teacher too, for content assertiveness.

- Write a final version.

- Follow your teacher's instructions.

TIPS FOR LIFE

Ethics in life

1 Read the text and discuss with your classmates: how do you think ethics and bioethics relate to the Genome Project?

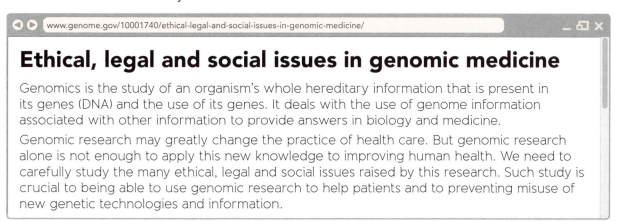

www.genome.gov/10001740/ethical-legal-and-social-issues-in-genomic-medicine/

Ethical, legal and social issues in genomic medicine

Genomics is the study of an organism's whole hereditary information that is present in its genes (DNA) and the use of its genes. It deals with the use of genome information associated with other information to provide answers in biology and medicine.

Genomic research may greatly change the practice of health care. But genomic research alone is not enough to apply this new knowledge to improving human health. We need to carefully study the many ethical, legal and social issues raised by this research. Such study is crucial to being able to use genomic research to help patients and to preventing misuse of new genetic technologies and information.

Available at: <www.genome.gov/10001740/ethical-legal-and-social-issues-in-genomic-medicine/>.
Accessed on: Mar. 19, 2019.

2 Break the code and write the message you are going to find out in your notebook.

A	B	C	D	E	F	G	H	I	K	N	O	R	S	T	U	V	W	Y
1	2	3	4	5	6	7	8	9	10	11	12	13	14	15	16	17	18	19

5 15 8 9 3 14   9 14   10 11 12 18 9 11 7   15 8 5

4 9 6 6 5 13 5 11 3 5   2 5 13 18 5 5 11   18 8 1 15

19 12 16   8 1 17 5   1   13 9 7 8 15   15 12   4 12   1 11 4

18 8 1 15   9 14   13 9 7 8 15   15 12   4 12

Potter Stewart

CHECK YOUR PROGRESS	😃	😐	🙁
Genetics			
Indefinite/Definite articles			
Relative pronouns			
Linking words			
Listening			
Speaking			
Reading			
Writing			

Luxy/Getty Images

1 Look at the picture and discuss with your classmates.

    a. What kinds of relationship do you see represented in the picture?

    b. What types of relationship do you have in your life?

    c. In your opinion, why are relationships important?

2 Read and listen to the dialog. Then act out.

40 **Allan:** Hi, Carol! How are you?

Carol: Good! Are you going to Kitty's party tonight?

Allan: No, I can't… I have an important Portuguese test tomorrow.

Carol: Oh, come on! Don't push yourself too hard! You're a very good student.

Allan: Yes, I am! But it's important to me. It's part of a bigger plan, you know?

Carol: What I know is you have a crush on Patti, and she will be there.

Allan: Really? I don't believe that! She never goes to parties!

Carol: That's exactly why I think you must go to the party. It's just one day. I can't see the problem!

Allan: Carol, have you ever dedicated your time to doing something special?

Carol: I'm not sure if I understand what you're saying…

Allan: I have studied Portuguese a lot because I want to spend one year in Mozambique as a volunteer, helping people in need.

Carol: I see… Sorry, Allan! I didn't know about that!

Allan: That's OK! But keep in mind: when I say no, it means no. Alright?

Carol: Yes, sure! There will be other parties you can go to!

3 Read the dialog again. Then write **T** (true) or **F** (false).

    a. ◯ Allan likes Patti in a romantic way.

    b. ◯ Allan can't go to the party because he is sick.

    c. ◯ Carol is going to a party in Kitty's house tonight.

    d. ◯ Allan wants to be a volunteer in Asia.

THINKING AHEAD

1 Have you ever heard the term *peer pressure*? If so, what do you know about it? If not, what do you think it is about? Talk to your classmates.

2 Read the text below. Were you right about the meaning of *peer pressure*? Share with your classmates.

3 Read the text again and write the following subtitles in the correct blanks.

> But, there is also positive peer pressure!   How do peers pressure?
>
> How do I resist peer pressure?

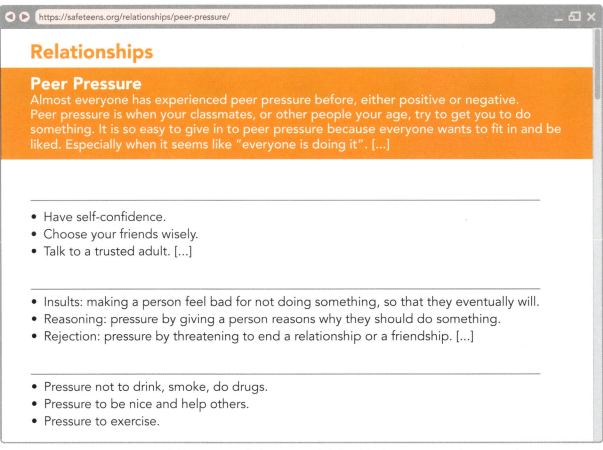

https://safeteens.org/relationships/peer-pressure/

Relationships

Peer Pressure
Almost everyone has experienced peer pressure before, either positive or negative. Peer pressure is when your classmates, or other people your age, try to get you to do something. It is so easy to give in to peer pressure because everyone wants to fit in and be liked. Especially when it seems like "everyone is doing it". [...]

_____

- Have self-confidence.
- Choose your friends wisely.
- Talk to a trusted adult. [...]

_____

- Insults: making a person feel bad for not doing something, so that they eventually will.
- Reasoning: pressure by giving a person reasons why they should do something.
- Rejection: pressure by threatening to end a relationship or a friendship. [...]

_____

- Pressure not to drink, smoke, do drugs.
- Pressure to be nice and help others.
- Pressure to exercise.

Available at: <https://safeteens.org/relationships/peer–pressure/>. Accessed on: Mar. 19, 2019.

4 Discuss the questions in groups. Then share your ideas with the whole class.

a. Is peer pressure always negative? Explain and give some examples.

b. What would you say to a peer who is pressuring you to do things you are not comfortable with?

c. What kind of advice would you give a friend who is behaving dangerously only because he/she wants to be accepted by certain members of the group?

A WORD WORK

 1 Listen and say. Then check how your friends make you feel.

41

glad

unhappy

hopeful

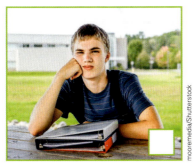

bored

anxious

confused

frustrated

embarrassed

insecure

guilty

shocked

confident

2 Complete the sentences below with the appropriate words from activity 1.

a. Patti told her parents a white lie and now she is feeling _____.

b. Robert can't sleep. He has a job interview this week, so he is very _____.

c. Rose has an English test on Tuesday. As she studied a lot, she is feeling

_____.

d. Carlos is _____. He doesn't have enough money to go to the concert.

3 In pairs, read the sentences and match each phrasal verb to its appropriate meaning.

I.

Did you know that Anna (a) **broke up** with Andre?

He (b) **cheated on** her! Can you believe that? He was seeing Sarah at the same time.

II.

I'm very happy we (c) **made up**.

Let's not fight anymore!

III.

Mary can no longer (d) **put up** with Joey, he has been very jealous.

They will (e) **split up** for sure.

IV.

Mike has been (f) **flirting with** Andrea for a long time. He sent her flowers yesterday.

So romantic! And it can actually (g) **work out**, I know she has a crush on him.

Ilustrações: Filipe Rocha/Arquivo da editora

○ to tolerate
○ to succeed
○ be dishonest

○ to end a relationship
○ to show romantic interest in someone
○ to forgive someone after an argument

LANGUAGE TIPS

A phrasal verb consists of a main verb with a particle (preposition, adverb or both) – the meaning of which is different from the meaning of its separate parts.

TIME FOR A GAME

Let's play **Mime** and **Brainstorming**!

Based on: <https://en.oxforddictionaries.com/grammar/phrasal-verbs>.
Accessed on: Mar. 22, 2019.

FOCUS ON LANGUAGE

1 Read the cartoon, paying attention to the highlighted words. Then check the correct option.

> I'VE FALLEN IN LOVE WITH YOUR VOICE, BUT UNFORTUNATELY, THINGS CAN PROBABLY NEVER WORK OUT BETWEEN US. I'M A CARTOON, AND YOU'RE A RECORDING.

2-5   UNIVERSAL UCLICK © 2015 J.C. DUFFY

© 2015 The Fusco Brothers, J. C. Duffy/Distr. by Andrews McMeel Syndication

a. ◯ The man fell in love in the past and is not in love anymore.

b. ◯ The man fell in love in the past and is still in love.

have = 've ⟶	**They've** been to Thailand.
has = 's ⟶	**She's** been to her friend's house.

2 Read the chart. Then underline the correct options to complete the statements about the Present Perfect.

Present Perfect								
Affirmative			**Interrogative**			**Negative**		
I	have		Have	I		I	haven't	
You	have		Have	you		You	haven't	
He	has		Has	he		He	hasn't	
She	has	fallen in love.	Has	she	fallen in love?	She	hasn't	fallen in love.
It	has		Has	it		It	hasn't	
We	have		Have	we		We	haven't	
You	have		Have	you		You	haven't	
They	have		Have	they		They	haven't	

a. We use the auxiliary verb **have/has** with *he, she, it*.

b. We use the auxiliary verb **have/has** with *I, you, we, they*.

c. We use the main verb in the **Simple Past/Past Participle** form.

GRAMMAR HELPER

Go to page 173.

3 Complete the sentences with **has/hasn't** or **have/haven't**.

a. Sarah and Paul _____ been together for five years. They plan to get married soon.

b. Allie and Sam _____ been to Jamaica yet. They went to Peru last summer.

c. Anna and I _____ studied in the same class since the first grade. We are BFF!

d. The library _____ been closed since last month. It _____ been closed for a year!

4 Read and underline the correct verb form to complete each sentence.

a. We haven't **done/did/do** our Math homework yet. We are tired.

b. I have just **to call/called/call** my sister. I miss her so much.

c. I haven't **seen/saw/seeing** Maria for a long time. I hope she is fine.

d. Haven't you **watch/to watch/watched** the original *Lion King* movie yet?

5 Write sentences in the Present Perfect using the words given.

a. Luana/lose/her book. She can't find it.

_____

_____

b. Mike and Tom/be/to France/last month. It was amazing!

_____

_____

c. Our dog/be sick/for two weeks. We are worried about him.

_____

_____

d. Lucas/play online games/since he was a teenager. This is not good for him!

_____

_____

Ilustrações: Filipe Rocha/ Arquivo da editora

6 Read the example. Then write short answers according to the pictures.

> Have you ever seen a koala?
> Yes, I have./No, I haven't.

a.

Has John washed his car?

_____

b.

Has Linda done her homework?

_____

c.

Have Tim and Marcus just played tennis?

_____

d.

Has Oliver cleaned up his bathroom?

_____

Ilustrações: Fido Nesti/ Arquivo da editora

7 In pairs, answer the questions using the verbs in parentheses. Follow the example.

> Do you think _The Avengers_ is a good movie? (**see**)
> Yes, _The Avengers_ is the best movie I've ever seen.

a. Is BTS a cool K-pop band? (listen)

_____

b. Is Rio de Janeiro a beautiful city? (ever/visit)

_____

c. Is Monopoly a fun board game? (play)

_____

d. Is "Soneto da Fidelidade", by Vinicius de Moraes, a romantic poem? (hear)

_____

8 Read the examples in the chart. Then complete the items with the correct adverb.

Time Adverbs – Present Perfect	
A: Has she **ever** been to Greece?	**A:** Have you **ever** traveled abroad?
B: Yes, she has **already** been to Greece.	**B:** No, I've **never** traveled abroad.
A: Have they **already** eaten dinner?	**A:** Has he **already** woken up?
B: No, they haven't eaten dinner **yet**.	**B:** Yes, he has **just** woken up.

a. _____ is usually used in questions with the Present Perfect to ask if something happened at any time in the past.

b. _____ is used with the Present Perfect to say that something happened or was done before now.

c. _____ is used with the Present Perfect to say that something has not happened at any time.

d. _____ is used with the Present Perfect to say that something has not happened, but will probably happen in the future. It is used in questions and negative sentences.

e. _____ is used with the Present Perfect to say that something happened a short time ago.

9 Complete the sentences with **yet** or **already**.

a. I've _____ visited my best friend in Florida.

b. Paul and Jane haven't traveled to Canada _____.

c. Amanda hasn't answered Allan's love letters _____.

d. Have you _____ invited your friends to your farewell party?

10 Write sentences in the Present Perfect using the words given and **just** or **ever**.

a. Polly/arrive at school

_____

b. you/see snow fall?

_____

c. Jamie/visit his relatives/in Japan?

_____

LISTEN AND SPEAK

1 Listen to two dialogs. What are they?

42

a. ◯ They're video calls.

b. ◯ They're phone calls.

c. ◯ They're face to face conversations.

2 Listen to the first dialog and answer the following questions. Then compare your answers
43 in pairs.

a. Who is Lane talking to?

_____

b. Who is Paula?

_____

c. Why does Juan seem worried about Paula?

_____

_____

d. What does Juan suggest doing on Saturday?

_____

_____

e. Why did Lane have to hang up?

_____

_____

3 Listen to the second dialog and write **T** (true), **F** (false) or **NM** (not mentioned).
44

a. ◯ Paula is happy at the new school.

b. ◯ Paula got a good grade in Math.

c. ◯ Paula got a bad grade in Science.

d. ◯ Lane suggests they study together before going to the movies.

e. ◯ Paula, Lane and Juan are going to the movies at 3 p.m. on Saturday.

4 Discuss the following questions with your classmates and teacher.

a. Have you ever helped a friend? What did you do?

b. Do you think Lane and Juan are being good friends to Paula? Why (not)?

c. When a friend is facing a difficult situation, how can you help?

5 In pairs, ask and answer the questions below. Then, in your notebook, write three other questions to know more about him/her.

1. Have you ever been abroad? If so, where have you been to?	2. Have you ever been camping? If so, where did you go? Did you like it?	3. Have you ever traveled by plane or by ship? Which one did/would you prefer?
4. Have you ever ridden a horse? An elephant? A camel? A motorbike? Anything else?	5. Have you ever won a prize? A competition?	6. Have you ever visited a fortune teller? Did you believe him/her?
7. Have you ever spoken to a foreigner in English?	8. Have you ever done anything that you really regret? What?	9. Have you ever been to an amusement park? What were your favorite rides?

PRONUNCIATION CORNER

1 Listen to the jazz chant and act out.

🔊45

A: Oh, no! Where is Joe?

B: Nobody knows.

A: Where is Ray?

B: He is late, I'm afraid.

A: Joe, Joe, hello!

B: Look out the window. There he goes.

A: I know, a minute ago… What's the date, Ray?

B: It's the eighth of April. It's eight to eight.

A: OK. Let's have a break!

B: Thanks, but I'm afraid we're late.

A: We can't be afraid.

B: I know, but we are late.

A: Very late, dear!

Fido Nesti/Arquivo da editora

2 Listen to the sentences and practice them.

🔊46

A: What's the **da**te, **K**ate?

B: It's **A**pril, the **eigh**th.

A: Thanks, **K**ate!

A: Where's **P**oe?

B: He's with **M**oe.

A: **M**oe?

READ AND WRITE

Text 1

1 Reflect on the following questions and talk to a classmate.

   a. How important is friendship to you?   **b.** Are you a good friend? Why (not)?

2 Read the quotes and answer the questions that follow.

> "Walking with a friend in the dark is better than walking alone in the light."
>
> Helen Keller (1880-1968, American author, political activist and lecturer)
>
> "The language of friendship is not words but meanings."
>
> Henry David Thoreau (1817-1862, American poet and philosopher)
>
> "Friends are the siblings God never gave us."
>
> Mencius (372 b.C.-289 b.C., Chinese philosopher)
>
> "A real friend is one who walks in when the rest of the world walks out."
>
> Walter Winchell (1897-1972, American journalist)

Available at: <www.goodreads.com/quotes>. Accessed on: Mar. 18, 2019.

   a. In your opinion, what do these quotes mean?

   _____

   _____

   b. Which quote better describes the meaning of friendship to you? Why?

   _____

   _____

   c. Is there any quote that you disagree with? If so, which one? Why?

   _____

   _____

3 Read the quotes again and check what you can infer from them.

   a. ◯ Quotes can flow through time.

   b. ◯ They present an unquestionable truth.

   c. ◯ The sentences are taken from a text or speech.

   d. ◯ Words are chosen carefully in order to impact readers and listeners.

4 Think of an important friend and write some words about what he/she means to you. Then share your text with him/her.

5 Read the captions and match them to the pictures.

a. Having fun together. **b.** Helping a friend to do something.

c. Opening up with a true friend. **d.** Cheering up a friend.

6 Now, in pairs, talk about the situations in activity 5. Then choose the most interesting statement from the conversation and quote it below.

_____

_____

_____

_____

7 Read the sentences below and answer the questions.

> I. "I want to talk to you so bad, but I'm just going to sit here in hopes that you start the conversation first."
> II. "Just a simple 'hello' from your crush makes you smile like a fool."
> III. "I find pieces of you in every song I listen to."

Available at: <https://br.pinterest.com>. Accessed on: Mar. 12, 2019.

a. Which sentence…

◯ has a humorous tone?

◯ shows that the person is probably shy?

◯ says every song that he/she listens to reminds him/her of a special person?

b. These sentences express how some teenagers deal with having feelings for someone. In your opinion, is it hard to deal with feelings? Are friends important in this kind of situation? Why (not)?

_____

_____

Text 2

8 The poem in activity 9 is different from the ones we usually read. It is an **acrostic poem**. Read it quickly and check the best definition for it.

    a. ◯ A poem that has fourteen lines and a particular pattern of rhyme.

    b. ◯ A text, usually a poem, in which particular elements, such as the first letter of each line, spell a word or a phrase.

9 Read the acrostic and choose the correct words to complete the statements.

Our love

John Peter Read

L is for "laughter" we had along the way.
O is for "optimism" you gave me every day.
V is for "value" of being my best friend.
E is for "eternity," a love that has no end.

Available at: <www.familyfriendpoems.com/poem/our-love-8>. Accessed on: Mar. 18, 2019.

    a. The poetic persona has a _____ view of love.

        ◯ negative   ◯ positive

    b. The loved person is also the poetic persona's _____.

        ◯ best friend   ◯ old friend

    c. The poetic persona knows that the love he/she feels will _____.

        ◯ never end   ◯ eventually end

10 Now, think about the characteristics of this poem and write **T** (true) or **F** (false).

    a. ◯ An acrostic poem has always more than five lines.

    b. ◯ The word formed by this acrostic poem is "friend".

    c. ◯ This poem is rhymed. The words "friend" and "end" are examples of it.

    d. ◯ Acrostic poets use the letters of a word to create new words and sentences.

11 What is your opinion about the acrostic poem from activity 9? Justify your answer.

_____

_____

_____

12 Think of feelings that are common to us all, such as love, sadness, joy, fear, anger. You can also think of things that are important to you, such as friendship, family, peace, school. Choose one word related to it and follow the steps below to write an acrostic poem.

a. Start by writing the chosen word vertically.

b. The topic of the first letter can be a simple word or a phrase.

c. Use a dictionary or a thesaurus to look for definitions and synonyms.

d. Brainstorming can help you. For example, if you chose *friendship* as your topic, ask yourself: what does this word remind me of? (e.g.: partnership, loyalty, belief, love, sharing etc.).

e. Create a mind map with topic-related words.

f. You can use metaphors in sentences.

g. Write a draft in your notebook and show it to your teacher.

h. Do all the necessary adjustments and write it on the lines below.

i. Write a final version to be shared with others. If possible, use a beautiful and colorful paper.

j. Create an acrostic mural and invite other classmates, teachers and school staff to appreciate it.

_____

_____

_____

_____

_____

_____

_____

_____

_____

_____

_____

_____

_____

_____

13 Now, read your acrostic poem to your classmates and listen to theirs. Which one was your 187 favorite? Discuss with your classmates.

Relationship and respect

1 In pairs, read the quotes below. Then, share your thoughts about the topic.

Banco de imagens/Arquivo da editora

> "A great relationship is about two things, appreciating your similarities and respecting your differences."

Healthy relationships with people around you make your life better. Respect, trust, and understanding are essential elements for a true relationship.

Available at: <www.purelovequotes.com/author/anonymous/a-great-relationship-is-about-two-things/>.
Accessed on: Mar. 18, 2019.

2 Now, in groups, create a short dialog concerning **relationship and respect**.

_____

_____

_____

_____

_____

3 Act out the dialog and present it to your classmates.

CHECK YOUR PROGRESS			
Feelings and phrasal verbs			
Present Perfect and time adverbs			
Listening			
Speaking			
Reading			
Writing			

REVIEW

UNITS 5 AND 6

◀1 Complete the text with the articles **a**, **an** or **the**.

> www.ndss.org/Down-Syndrome/What-Is-Down-Syndrome/#sthash.ZCcBuET4.dpuf ― 🗖 ✕
>
> ### What Is Down Syndrome?
>
> […] Typically, _____ nucleus of each cell contains 23 pairs of chromosomes, half of which are inherited from each parent. Down syndrome occurs when _____ individual has _____ full or partial extra copy of chromosome 21.
>
> This additional genetic material alters _____ course of development and causes _____ characteristics associated with Down syndrome. A few of the common physical traits of Down syndrome are low muscle tone, small stature, _____ upward slant to the eyes, and _____ single deep crease across the center of _____ palm – although each person with Down syndrome is _____ unique individual and may possess these characteristics to different degrees, or not at all. […]

Available at: <www.ndss.org/Down-Syndrome/What-Is-Down-Syndrome/#sthash.ZCcBuET4.dpuf>.
Accessed on: Mar. 22, 2018.

◀2 Read the sentences and underline the correct relative pronoun.

  a. I go to school with a girl **who/which/where** is a professional actress.

  b. Here is the Science magazine **who/which/whose** I borrowed from you last week.

  c. Do you like the new house **where/who/whose** you live now?

  d. The family **who/which/where** lives across the street from us is from New Zealand.

  e. The neighborhood **where/which/who** Marcie goes to school is quite safe.

◀3 Circle the connector that best completes each sentence.

  a. I can't understand French, **but/and** I can speak English well.

  b. Stephanie can act **but/and** dance very well.

  c. I was tired last night, **so/however** I went to bed early.

  d. I'm not going out **why/because** I have a terrible cold.

4 Write sentences using the Present Perfect.

a. we/already/be/to India

_____

b. I/just/have dinner/with my parents

_____

c. Paul and Celine/not study/for the Geography test/yet

_____

d. John and Liz/never/eat *feijoada*

_____

e. Grandma/just/bake an apple pie

_____

5 Read the answers and write the questions.

a. **A:** _____
B: No, Patty hasn't done her homework yet.

b. **A:** _____
B: Yes, my aunt Julia has already found a job.

c. **A:** _____
B: Yes, I have been to the supermarket to buy some pears.

d. **A:** _____
B: Yes, they have been to Wellington and Auckland.

e. **A:** _____
B: No, Emily has never watched a western movie.

6 Give personal short answers.

a. Have you ever traveled abroad?

_____

b. Have you ever helped your mother cook dinner or set the table?

_____

c. Have you already had lunch?

_____

d. Have you already done your homework?

_____

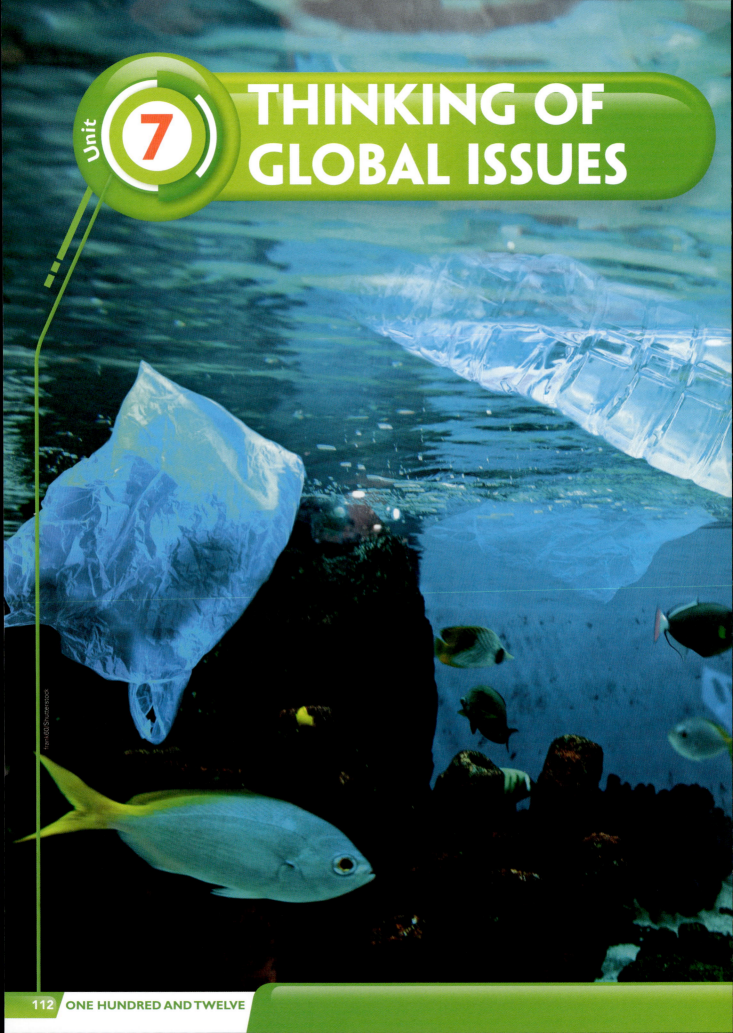

Unit 7

THINKING OF GLOBAL ISSUES

frank60/Shutterstock

1 Look at the picture, read the questions and discuss them with your classmates.

    a. What does the picture represent?

    b. Imagine how the world will be like in the future. Explain your point of view.

2 Read and listen to the dialog. Then act out.

47 **Kitty:** Hi, guys! What are you talking about?

Jim: We're talking about the School Cultural Week.

Allan: Have you attended all lectures?

Kitty: No, I haven't. I haven't had enough time yet.

Carol: I attended all of them. The topics were polemic and interesting: epidemic diseases, pollution, environment…

Jim: I only attended the one about epidemic diseases last Monday. It was very interesting!

Allan: And more will be discussed about epidemic diseases next week!

Kitty: I've read some news that epidemic diseases are spreading.

Leo: Yes, but people can prevent the spread of some infectious diseases by doing preventive medicine, having proper treatment and being well-informed.

Carol: I've heard about this program that has helped thousands of people since it started.

Jim: And what do you think about pollution?

Leo: I think it's serious, and it's also a huge teenage problem.

Kitty: In my opinion, there's so much to be done to resolve such big environmental problems we face now.

Allan: Let's go for a walk in the park and think of ways we can help save our planet.

Leo: And enjoy a milkshake?

Allan: Sure, Leo!

3 Answer the questions according to the dialog.

    a. What topics were discussed in the School Cultural Week lectures?

    b. How can people prevent the spread of some diseases?

THINKING AHEAD

1 We live in a world with poverty, diseases, gender inequality, environmental problems etc. Fortunately, there are inspiring young people who have powerful ideas and contribute to their communities and to the environment. Do you know any of them?

2 Read the text about Shelby and answer the following questions.

https://barronprize.org/meet-the-winners/2018-winners/

Shelby

Founder, Jr Ocean Guardians

Age at Winning Prize: 17

Home State: California

Additional Media Coverage: Fearless Fabulous You – 11/14/18

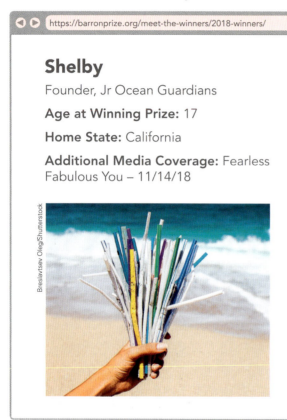

Breslavtsev Oleg/Shutterstock

Shelby founded Jr Ocean Guardians, a non-profit that educates young children about plastic pollution and the ways they can protect our oceans and planet. She created an activity book for elementary students, including a Spanish edition, that she has distributed in classrooms to more than 1,000 children. She also created the #NoStrawNovember movement, requesting and receiving a statewide No Straw November Resolution from the California Coastal Commission. Her No Straw November movement has garnered more than 10,000 straw-free pledges on her social media sites from people in over 20 countries. Shelby is currently working on straw-free legislation, teaming with the Monterey Bay Aquarium and testifying at the California State Capitol in support of a bill to eliminate plastic straws statewide [...].

Available at: <https://barronprize.org/meet-the-winners/2018-winners/>. Accessed on: Mar. 19, 2019.

a. What is the objective of Shelby's Jr Ocean Guardians organization?

_____

b. What movement has Shelby created?

_____

c. If you had the chance, what would you do to help your community or the environment?

_____

TO LEARN MORE

To see other outstanding young leaders, go to: <https://barronprize.org/meet-the-winners/2018-winners/>. Accessed on: Mar. 19, 2019.

A WORD WORK

1 48 Let's think of some health, social and environmental issues. They are part of our daily lives.

Health Issues

epidemic diseases

addiction

Social Issues

violence

poverty

unemployment

racism

hunger

war

Environmental Issues

tornadoes

floods

earthquakes

droughts

pollution

water shortage

2 Do some research and, in your notebook, list three problems the world faces nowadays.

3 Match the nouns from the box to their definitions.

| addiction   epidemic diseases   drought   hunger   earthquake |

a. (_____) a series of vibrations induced in the Earth's crust by the abrupt rupture of rocks.

b. (_____) diseases that rapidly spread to a large number of people in a given population.

c. (_____) condition of being addicted to a particular substance, thing or activity, facing difficulties to stop without help.

d. (_____) a shortage of food.

e. (_____) a long period of dry weather.

TIME FOR A GAME

Let's play **What's missing?** and **Word list!**

4 Read and discuss with a classmate.

a. In your opinion, what brings violence to the world?

b. Name three actions that could be taken to make the world more peaceful and fair.

c. Is education important to put these actions into practice? Why (not)?

FOCUS ON LANGUAGE

◀1 In pairs, read the article fragment below, then answer orally: what has caused an increase in world hunger?

> http://theconversation.com/world-hunger-has-risen-for-three-straight-years-and-climate-change-is-a-cause-103818
>
> ## World hunger **has risen** for **three straight years, and climate change is a cause**
> October 22, 2018 6.40am EDT
>
> World hunger has risen **for** a third consecutive year, according to the United Nations' annual food security report. The total number of people who face chronic food deprivation has increased by 15 million **since** 2016. [...]

Available at: <http://theconversation.com/world-hunger-has-risen-for-three-straight-years-and-climate-change-is-a-cause-103818>. Accessed on: Mar. 5, 2019.

◀2 Pay attention to the words in **bold** in the fragment above. Then complete the chart.

Present Perfect with *for* and *since*	
Duration (from start to end)	**A point from the past until now**
World hunger was risen **for** a third consecutive year [...]	The total people who face chronic food deprivation has increased by 15 million **since** 2016.
John has lived in Boston ___ two weeks.	Liz has worked _____ 7 a.m.

◀3 Fill in the gaps with **hasn't worked** or **didn't work**.

Present Perfect × Simple Past	
He _____ on Saturdays for two months.	He _____ last Saturday.

◀4 Complete the text about Tom using the Simple Past or the Present Perfect.

Tom _____ (be) to many countries around the world lately. He _____ (start) traveling in 1985. He _____ (visit) over twenty countries since then. He _____ (travel) to Europe in 1991 and to South America in 1993. His favorite city is Lima, in Peru. He _____ (spend) three months there in 1994. Then, he _____ (go) back to New Delhi, India, last week.

GRAMMAR HELPER

Go to page 175.

5 Underline the correct words to complete the sentences.

a. Allan will start a research project on social issues **tomorrow/two weeks ago/ever**.

b. They are attending the lecture **one month ago/yesterday/now**.

c. I met her **two weeks ago/already/since** at the library.

d. Have you **never/already/now** finished your exercises?

e. Bill has **yesterday/for/never** been to the city zoo.

f. We haven't finished the lesson **just/yet/never**.

g. My grandpa hasn't worked **for/just/since** 1998.

h. Jim **attended/has attended** a lecture on environmental issues last Friday.

i. Last week, my parents and I **saw/have seen** the latest Tom Cruise movie.

j. Mary has looked for a cheaper house **since/for/yet** a long time. Then, she gave up.

6 Read the box below, then complete the questions according to the answers.

noomie103/Shutterstock

> ### Simple Past + ago
>
> Marion **attended** the lecture one week **ago**.
> I **took** the same course two years **ago**.

a. What _____?
   Ms. Jones taught us a lesson about epidemic diseases two days ago.

b. How _____?
   The weather was very sunny yesterday.

c. What _____?
   I bought a beautiful dress last week.

d. When _____?
   My friends and I traveled around Europe last month.

e. Where _____?
   I went to Grace's house last Saturday.

f. Who _____?
   Frank went to a lecture last Monday.

7 Answer the questions using the words in parentheses.

a. Has Paul met his girlfriend? (last Monday)

_____

b. Have you heard the latest news? (ten minutes ago)

_____

c. Have you finished your school project? (yesterday)

_____

d. Have the students had Math classes? (in the morning)

_____

8 Complete the dialog using the appropriate forms of the verbs from the box.

start	do	learn	be (2x)	have

Carol: Sorry, guys, am I late?

Kitty: Yes, you are, Carol. We've

_____ here for a long time.

Carol: I'm really sorry. But I'm late because I was watching a TV program about Stefanie Lacy, a Barron Prize winner.

Leo: Why _____ she win it?

Carol: Because she _____ a successful recycling program in her town.

Kitty: That's cool. What about doing something like that here?

Leo: Our town already

_____ a recycling program. We could start a program to help others.

Carol: Good idea! I _____ that good deeds for the world can

_____ done by everyone.

Filipe Rocha/Arquivo da editora

9 Read the examples from the chart and write **AV** (active voice) or **PV** (passive voice).

a. ◯ The subject performs an action; the emphasis is on the subject.

b. ◯ An action is performed by a subject (which can be omitted); the emphasis is on the action.

Active Voice (AV) × Passive Voice (PV)
I teach the lesson. (AV)
The lesson is taught by me. (PV)
Bruno wrote the e-mail. (AV)
The e-mail was written by Bruno. (PV)
They will discuss the problems. (AV)
The problems will be discussed (by them). (PV)

GRAMMAR HELPER

Go to page 175.

10 Read the chart from activity 9 again and complete the sentences below using Passive Voice.

a. This Chinese industry processes fresh food.

Fresh food _____ by this Chinese industry.

b. My teacher corrected all the tests about floods.

All the tests about floods _____ by my teacher.

c. Scientists will study about droughts around the world.

Droughts around the world _____ by scientists.

11 Read and circle the appropriate words to complete the sentences.

a. The windows **were washed/was washed** in spite of water shortage.

b. The school **will paint/will be painted** next month. We will have a cultural event.

c. The school program about pollution and global warming **was seen/seen** by the scientists.

d. I **found/was found** a black schoolbag at the park yesterday.

e. A new scientific documentary **will be produced/will produce** by that famous director.

LISTEN AND SPEAK

1 What do you know about Zika virus? Read the paragraph below and talk to a classmate. Then take notes about it.

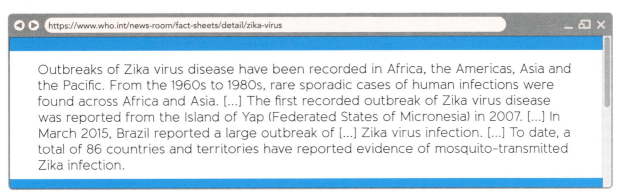

https://www.who.int/news-room/fact-sheets/detail/zika-virus

Outbreaks of Zika virus disease have been recorded in Africa, the Americas, Asia and the Pacific. From the 1960s to 1980s, rare sporadic cases of human infections were found across Africa and Asia. [...] The first recorded outbreak of Zika virus disease was reported from the Island of Yap (Federated States of Micronesia) in 2007. [...] In March 2015, Brazil reported a large outbreak of [...] Zika virus infection. [...] To date, a total of 86 countries and territories have reported evidence of mosquito-transmitted Zika infection.

Available at: <https://www.who.int/news-room/fact-sheets/detail/zika-virus>. Accessed on: Mar. 5, 2019.

2 **49** You are going to listen to a reporter talking about Zika virus infection. Listen once and decide which topics related to the disease she mentions.

- **a.** ◯ The way the disease first appeared.
- **b.** ◯ Symptoms and transmission.
- **c.** ◯ The spread of the disease in the world today.
- **d.** ◯ Treatment and prevention.

3 **50** Listen again and write **T** (true) or **F** (false), then compare your answers in pairs.

- **a.** ◯ The disease is only transmitted by mosquito bites.
- **b.** ◯ This mosquito can also cause other diseases.
- **c.** ◯ Fever and headache are symptoms of the Zika infection.
- **d.** ◯ Unborn babies can develop microcephaly, and in adults and children the infection can cause neurological disorders.
- **e.** ◯ The disease cannot be diagnosed by laboratory tests.
- **f.** ◯ The best way to prevent the disease is avoiding mosquito bites.

4 **51** How can we prevent the reproduction of the mosquitoes? Listen again and come up with some other ideas in pairs.

TO LEARN MORE

Watch the video Zika Virus: What We Know (And What We Don't) published by Sci Show News, available at: <https://www.youtube.com/watch?v=JUlGN5XJ5dc>. Accessed on: Mar. 3, 2019.

5 Listen to the dialog below, then practice it with a classmate using the following information.

🔊 52

> see the latest documentary about earthquakes/two weeks ago

Jim: Have you seen the latest documentary about earthquakes?

Leo: Yes, I have.

Jim: When did you see it?

Leo: I saw it two weeks ago.

a. join in our campaign against poverty/five days ago

b. recycle cans/last night

c. visit your grandmother recently/last Saturday

d. listen to that radio program about addictions/yesterday

PRONUNCIATION CORNER

1 Listen and act out the jazz chant.

🔊 53

A: Do you like flying a kite?
B: Yes, it's very exciting!
A: What about climbing?
B: I prefer bicycle riding.

A: I can't stand this spoilt boy.
He speaks in a loud voice.
He has a big and noisy toy.
That makes an awful noise!

A: Hey, boy! Stop shouting!
Hey, boy! You... sit down.
Now... turn it down,
Or... I'll throw it out! Ouch!

Fido Nesti/Arquivo da editora

2 Listen and practice the words.

🔊 54

> noisy shout kite toy ouch high

3 Write them in the correct column, according to their sounds.

/aɪ/	/aʊ/	/ɔɪ/
price	couch	choice

READ AND WRITE

Text 1

1 The infographic below is about how to prevent diseases caused by bug bites. In pairs, discuss the following questions and take notes. Share them with your classmates.

a. Besides Zika, what other diseases can bug bites cause to humans?

b. What would you do to prevent them?

2 Read the infographic and find the following information in it.

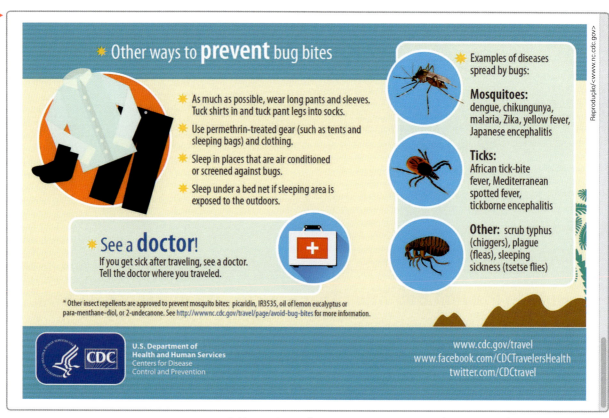

Available at: <https://www.everydayhealth.com/infographics/how-prevent-bug-bites-spread-zika-other-diseases/>. Accessed on: Mar. 19, 2019.

a. The sentence which sums up the threat: _____

b. Ways to prevent the diseases: _____

c. What to do in case of insect bites: _____

3 Check the best alternative to complete each sentence.

a. The infographic aims mainly at _____.
   ○ doctors   ○ travelers

b. The species of bugs which mainly threatens people are _____.
   ○ mosquitoes, fleas and ticks.   ○ all kinds of bugs.

c. _____ can protect you effectively from bug bites.
   ○ Repellents   ○ Sunscreen

d. Wearing _____ can help avoid bites.
   ○ short pants and long sleeves   ○ long pants and sleeves

4 Besides sharing infographics, what else can be done in order to help protect travelers?

Text 2

5 Read the dictionary definition below. What other natural disasters can you think of? Tell your classmates.

tsunami noun

: a great sea wave produced especially by submarine earth movement or volcanic eruption

Available at: <www.merriam-webster.com/dictionary/tsunami>.
Accessed on: Mar. 19, 2019.

6 Read the news report below. Then check the consequences of it.

https://www.theguardian.com/world/2018/dec/24/sunda-strait-tsunami-volcano-indonesia

Indonesia tsunami caused by collapse of volcano

Expert confirmation comes as officials say country needs new tsunami early warning system

The deadly tsunami in Indonesia was triggered by a chunk of the Anak Krakatau volcano slipping into the ocean, officials have confirmed, amid calls for a new early warning system that can detect volcanic eruptions.

At least 373 people were killed and many buildings were heavily damaged when the tsunami struck, almost without warning, along the rim of the Sunda Strait between Java and Sumatra islands late on Saturday. [...]

Nurul Hidayat/Bisnis Indonesia/Associated Press/ Glow Images

The fact that the tsunami was triggered by a volcano rather than an earthquake meant no tsunami warning was triggered, scientists said. Coastal residents reported not seeing or feeling any warning signs before waves of up to three metres high surged in.

Hundreds of military personnel and volunteers spent Monday scouring beaches strewn with debris in search of survivors. At least 1,459 people were injured and more than 600 homes, 60 shops and 420 vessels damaged when the tsunami struck. [...].

The water washed away an outdoor stage where a local rock band, Seventeen, were performing, killing their bassist and manager. Other people who had been watching the band on the beach were missing.

Azki Kurniawan, 16, said his first warning about the tsunami was when people burst into the lobby of the Patra Comfort hotel shouting: "Sea water rising."

Kurniawan, who was undergoing vocational training with a group of 30 other students, said he was confused because he had not felt a big earthquake. He said he ran to the car park to try to reach his motorbike but discovered it was already flooded.

"Suddenly, a one-metre wave hit me," he said, his eyes red and swollen from crying. "I was thrown into the fence of a building about 30 metres from the beach and held on to the fence as strong as I could, trying to resist the water, which felt like it would drag me back into the sea. I cried in fear... 'This is a tsunami?' I was afraid I would die."

Available at: <https://www.theguardian.com/world/2018/dec/24/sunda-strait-tsunami-volcano-indonesia>. Accessed on: Mar. 19, 2019.

a. ◯ At least 373 people died.

b. ◯ Many buildings and houses collapsed or were damaged.

c. ◯ The country had no early warning system.

d. ◯ More than 1,400 people were injured.

e. ◯ The tsunami triggered an earthquake.

f. ◯ The manager and the bassist of the band Seventeen died.

◀7 Answer the questions according to the text.

a. What caused the disaster?

_____

b. What could have avoided so many losses?

_____

◀8 Complete the sentences below about some characteristics of the text genre news report using words from the box.

body   attention   credibility   impersonal   past tense   written

a. A news report can be _____ or spoken.

b. The text is simple, concise, precise and _____.

c. The text is written in the _____.

d. Pictures are used to grab reader's _____.

e. A news report consists basically in three parts: the headline, the lead and the

_____.

f. Direct quotations are used to provide strengh and _____.

◀9 What about being a journalist for one day? Write a news report about something that has
189 happened in your neighborhood or in your school. Follow the steps below.

a. Collect information and some quotes of people who were involved in the facts.

b. Find answers to the questions: "What?", "When?", "Where?", "Who?" and "How?".

c. Look for some pictures to grab readers' attention.

d. Write a draft, check the grammar and the spelling.

e. Show it to the teacher and make the necessary adjustments.

f. Write a final version and publish it on the school website or blog.

TIPS FOR LIFE

Global Issues

◀1 Look at the graphic and discuss it with your classmates. Then make a collaborative panel.

Global concerns

Average percentage share of concern for the following issues facing the world out of 17 countries worldwide

Global terrorism	25.1
Poverty, hunger, thirst	15.2
Climate change	12.8
Armed conflicts	10.6
Economic instability	10.0
Population growth	7.0
Spread of diseases	6.1
Energy scarcity	5.3
Nuclear weapons	4.8

YouGov | yougov.com

January 2016

◀2 Read the quote and discuss: do you agree with it? Justify your answer.

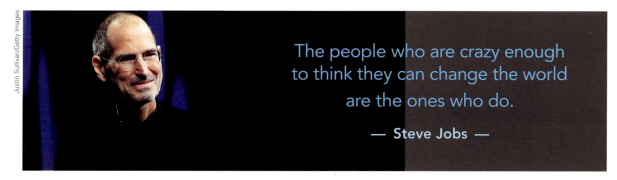

The people who are crazy enough to think they can change the world are the ones who do.

— Steve Jobs —

CHECK YOUR PROGRESS

	😃	😐	🙁
Human Issues Concern			
Present Perfect (for, since)			
Simple Past + ago			
Active × Passive Voice			
Listening			
Speaking			
Reading			
Writing			

bluedog studio/Shutterstock

1 Look at the picture and discuss with your classmates.

    a. How is pollution affecting the environment of your city?

    b. What are the most urgent environmental issues today?

2 Read and listen to the dialog. Then act out.

55 **Leo:** Where are you going, Carol?

Carol: I'm going home.

Leo: Can I come with you? I need to talk to Jim.

Carol: Sure, Leo.

Leo: Did you go out on Sunday morning?

Carol: Yes, I went to a meeting about environmental issues. My friends belong to an organization called Water Planet. Biodiversity is in danger! If we don't do anything, many species of animals and plants will disappear in a few years.

Leo: You've already been to the rainforest meetings, haven't you?

Carol: Yes, I have. I'm also collecting articles about global warming. They've said that even if the emissions of greenhouse gases were stopped today, it would take thousands of years to go back to pre-industrial levels. So, there is much work to be done! We have to act now!

Leo: I've read about it. Human activity is putting more and more gases into the air. I didn't know you were so interested in environmental issues, Carol!

Carol: Yes, I am. I've grown up, Leo! I'm not just Jim's little sister anymore. I have my own opinion and fight for important causes.

3 Answer the questions.

    a. What kind of environmental issues were mentioned in the dialog?

    _____

    b. What is the greenhouse effect?

    _____

    c. What can be done to preserve the environment?

    _____

1 Read the book cover and answer the questions.

The Young Activist's Guide to

BUILDING A GREEN MOVEMENT + CHANGING THE WORLD

PLAN A CAMPAIGN / RECRUIT SUPPORTERS
LOBBY POLITICIANS / PASS LEGISLATION
RAISE MONEY / ATTRACT MEDIA ATTENTION

Sharon J. Smith
Program advisor of Earth Island Institute's Brower Youth Awards
Foreword by JULIA BUTTERFLY HILL

a. What is the title of the book?

_____

_____

b. Who is the author?

_____

c. What does the book cover mention about her?

_____

_____

d. What is this book about?

_____

_____

_____

2 Read the quote and the clues given to discover who the mystery person is.

"At first, I thought that I was struggling to save rubber trees, then I thought that I was struggling to save the Amazon rainforest. Now, I realize I am fighting for humanity."

CLUE 1: He was a conservationist, born in Xapuri, Acre, Brazil, on December 15th, 1944.

CLUE 2: He actively participated in the struggles of the rubber tappers to prevent deforestation and the indiscriminate cutting down of rubber trees. He was an environmental activist.

CLUE 3: On December 22nd, 1988, he was murdered at his home because he was fighting for a better world.

a. Who was he?

_____

b. Have you heard about him before doing this activity? Share what you know about him with your classmates.

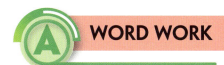

WORD WORK

1 Green practices! Let's care for the environment. Look at the pictures and listen. Then say **56** the words.

reforestation

depollution of rivers

protection of riverbanks

soil restoration

erosion control

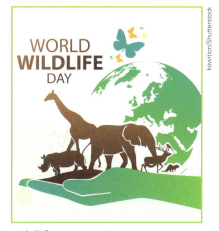

wildlife protection programs

metal recycling

glass recycling

electronic recycling

paper recycling

plastic recycling

rubber recycling

2 Find and circle seven words in the word search. Then use them to complete the following sentences.

R	E	F	O	R	E	S	T	A	T	I	O	N	G	A	R	M	D
V	M	E	T	Y	U	I	O	P	X	B	V	I	H	A	E	D	E
M	V	L	P	O	G	F	A	S	U	Y	I	M	R	H	S	L	P
E	R	O	S	I	O	N	J	A	R	O	F	E	E	M	T	K	O
H	S	M	G	I	E	R	A	S	Y	U	O	V	C	E	O	A	L
W	I	L	D	L	I	F	E	P	L	K	J	H	Y	U	R	O	L
M	R	U	N	O	R	E	X	A	T	O	I	U	C	W	A	T	U
R	R	I	V	E	R	B	A	N	K	S	T	O	L	S	T	U	T
V	F	P	X	B	V	I	M	S	T	U	I	P	I	P	I	K	I
G	V	A	I	D	S	G	H	K	L	P	O	I	N	E	O	Y	O
F	G	H	N	M	L	P	S	W	E	R	B	M	G	S	N	T	N

a. _____ is treating or processing used or waste material to make them suitable for reuse.

b. The goal of soil _____ is to minimize its degradation.

c. Protection of _____ with native vegetation can improve water quality.

d. _____ control is the practice of preventing or controlling wind or water erosion on the surface of the Earth.

e. _____ of rivers can restore freshwater environments.

f. _____ is the process of restoring and recreating areas of woodlands or forests that once existed but have been deforested.

g. _____ protection programs lead efforts to protect endangered species.

TIME FOR A GAME

Let's play **Hangman** and **Scrambled words**!

1 Read the sentences from the dialog on page 129 and match them to the ideas they express.

  a. "If we don't do anything, many species of animals and plants will disappear in a few years."

  b. "[...] if the emissions of greenhouse gases were stopped today, it would take thousands of years to go back to pre-industrial levels."

  ◯ It presents a hypothetical/unreal situation.

  ◯ It presents a real possible situation.

2 Read the chart and complete it with the missing information.

First Conditional (real and possible situations)
If + Simple Present + will + main verb
If I **have** money, I **will** travel to London.
Sometimes we can use first conditional with modal verbs: **can**, **may**, **must**.
If + Simple Present + can/may/must + main verb

If it _____ raining, we **can** play soccer.

If you _____ a better world, you **must** become a conscious consumer.

Second Conditional (unreal or impossible situations)
If + Simple Past + would + main verb
If I **were** rich, I **would** travel to Europe and Asia.
Sometimes we can use second conditional with modal verbs: **could**, **should**, **might**.
If + Simple Past + could/should/might + main verb

If I _____ 20 years younger, I **could** go back to college.

If Dave _____ to his friend, she **might** help him.

3 Read the example below and, using the First Conditional, write sentences about what you can do to help protect planet Earth.

GRAMMAR HELPER

Go to page 176.

  a. If you turn the lights off, you will save energy.

  b. _____

  c. _____

  d. _____

4 Match the columns to create sentences in the Second Conditional.

a. If I were the mayor,

b. If he studied more,

c. We would do more things to help the environment

d. If she were older,

◯ he would have better grades.

◯ I would protect the environment.

◯ she would travel alone.

◯ if we could.

5 Choose the correct alternative to complete each sentence.

a. If there is a green campaign at my school,

◯ I will join it.

◯ my teacher will buy it.

◯ I would join it.

b. If I want to feel better,

◯ I must eat healthy food.

◯ I was eating healthy food.

◯ I might eat healthy food.

c. If we don't do anything about the environment now,

◯ we should live better.

◯ we used to do it.

◯ we will pay for it in the future.

d. If people don't save water,

◯ we would buy it.

◯ we are concerned people.

◯ we will have a great problem in the future.

e. If gorillas aren't protected,

◯ they will disappear.

◯ they are very big.

◯ they could live more.

f. If you want to go with me to the Green Meeting,

◯ I should go there.

◯ I will get the tickets.

◯ I will stay here.

6 Complete the sentences below to make them true about you. Use the First and the Second Conditionals.

a. If I don't study, _____

b. If I eat a lot of junk food, _____

c. If I don't drink water, _____

d. If I were the president, _____

e. If I won the lottery, _____

f. If I could travel to the future, _____

7 Posters are usually simple: there is a small amount of text and a title written in large font size. Sometimes a poster does not have any text, but in this case its image has to be strong enough to deliver the message. Read the poster below and answer the questions.

OUR PLANET IS WHAT WE MAKE OF IT.

Do your part by properly disposing of your trash and recyclables, and together we can help prevent the planet from going to waste.

Visit
www.GREENPROJECT.org
to find out more about how you can help.

a. Is the image part of the message in the poster? Why (not)?

_____

_____

b. Do you agree with the title "Our Planet is What We Make of It."? Why (not)? Explain your point of view.

_____

_____

c. What have you done to protect the environment lately? Explain it in a few words.

_____

_____

8 How green are you? Take the quiz and find out!

Questions	Yes	No
a. If you are with a group of friends in a park and they throw garbage on the ground, will you ask them to throw it in the waste bin?		
b. If a woman standing close to you in a store wanted to buy a fur coat, would you ask her to change her mind and buy something else instead?		
c. If your brother/sister forgets to turn off the lights, will you do it yourself?		
d. If your best friend had been in the shower for more than 10 minutes, would you ask him/her to stop wasting water?		
e. If your parents have an old car which pollutes the air, will you ask them to have it fixed?		

Score

Yes = 5 points
No = 1 point

The higher you score, the greener you are!

9 Read the cartoon and answer the following questions.

YOUR TRANSLATION IS FINE. BUT **ACTUAL** IS NOT THE SAME AS ALTUAL, **AUDIENCE** IS NOT AUDIENCIA, AND **CASUALIDADES** IS NOT...

a. What is the importance of knowing the meaning of false friends or false cognates?

b. Give an example of an embarrassing situation that could happen due to improper use of a false friend.

10 In pairs, read the sentences from the chart. Then, write synonyms for the false friends using a dictionary.

False Friends	Synonyms
You don't know the **actual** reason that made me cry.	real, true
Only after graduating from high school, I will think about what to do in **college**.	_____
I'll go to the **costume** party wearing a big, colored hat.	_____
Please, could you show me the main **exit** from this building?	_____
The book is available at the school **library**.	_____
I traveled to Salvador with my **parents** and my sister.	_____
Prejudice is one of the most stupid things in the world.	_____
Don't **pretend** to be sick! I know you're perfectly well.	_____
Grip the rope and climb up.	_____
Now I **realize** you are my best friend.	_____

LANGUAGE TIPS

False Cognates or **False Friends** are words that are similar in form, but have different meanings.

LISTEN AND SPEAK

1 What do you know about plastic pollution? Read 10 facts about it and share your opinion with your classmates: which fact is more interesting or shocking?

www.globalcitizen.org/en/content/plastic-pollution-facts/

Rich Carey/Shutterstock

1. Since the 1950s, around 8.3 billion tons of plastic have been produced worldwide.
2. In some parts of the world, using plastic is already illegal.
3. 73% of beach litter worldwide is plastic.
4. A million plastic bottles are bought around the world every minute.
5. Worldwide, about 2 million plastic bags are used every minute.
6. 90% of plastic polluting our oceans is carried by just 10 rivers.
7. Plastic is killing more than 1.1 million seabirds and animals every year.
8. The average person eats 70,000 microplastics each year.
9. The average time that a plastic bag is used for is... 12 minutes.
10. Over the past 50 years, world plastic production has doubled.

Available at: <www.globalcitizen.org/en/content/plastic–pollution–facts/>. Accessed on: Mar. 3, 2019.

2 You are going to listen to some facts about plastic pollution. Listen to it once and answer:
57 What kind of plastic pollution is the audio about?

_____

3 Listen again and check the sentence that is **not** true.
58

○ Charging a few cents for a plastic bag in stores and markets is an idea to encourage people to bring their own cloth bags when shopping.

○ Plastic bag pollution is not a big issue for planet Earth.

○ It's Black Friday in Canada. It's a famous sales day. People are carrying plastic bags home.

○ Governments all over the world are trying to make an effort to remove plastic bags from the environment.

TO LEARN MORE

Visit the Global Citizen website to read more about plastic pollution (<www.globalcitizen.org/en/content/plastic-pollution-facts/>; accessed on: Mar. 5, 2019). You can also watch the video *How we can keep plastics out of our oceans,* by National Geographic (<www.youtube.com/watch?v=HQTUWK7CM-Y>; accessed on: Mar. 5, 2019).

4 Discuss the questions with your classmates.

    a. What do you and your family do with plastic bags? Do you use them? How?

    b. Do you take your own bags when you go shopping? Why (not)?

5 In pairs, imagine you are members of the government and think of ways to reduce the use of plastic bags in your neighborhood. Then, share ideas with your classmates.

How to reduce the use of plastic bags

_____

_____

_____

_____

_____

_____

PRONUNCIATION CORNER

1 Listen to the jazz chant and act out.

🔊**59**

    A: Oh, sorry. I was allowed to talk aloud.
    B: And I was very weak last week.

    B: When I flew to L.A. I got a flu, this left me very bored on board.
    A: Poor girl! Yesterday, I ate at eight.

    A: I was very late and had a break.
    B: Yesterday, I asked about the weather, and whether I could go out in bad weather.

    A: Then, I rode my bike along a very long road.
    B: Sorry interrupting old toad, but someone told me... that Lou had asked for some flour, and they had brought her some flowers!

2 Listen and practice the homophones.

🔊**60**

    I was very **weak** last **week** due to the flu.
    Yesterday, I was late, I **ate** at **eight**.
    I went out to buy some **flour**, and I bought some **flowers**, too!

LANGUAGE TIPS

A **homophone** is a word that is pronounced the same way as another word, but differs in meaning and may differ in spelling.

READ AND WRITE

Text 1

1 In 2019, a big tragedy took place in Brumadinho, in Minas Gerais, Brazil. You are going to read a news report about it. What kind of information do you expect to read in the text? Talk to your classmates about it.

2 Read the news report and answer the question: If you could sum up this tragedy in one sentence, what would it be?

_____

_____

www.hello!teens.com/environment

Deadly Brazil dam collapse raises fears of environmental woes

Experts say the real long-term effects of the collapse of a dam at a mine near the Brazilian town of Brumadinho may not be evident for years.

A week after a dam storing mining waste collapsed in southeast Brazil, the human cost is clear, with 110 killed and 238 missing, presumed dead, but the environmental impact is still being evaluated.

Authorities fear the mineral-laced slurry released by the collapse could eventually pollute the Sao Francisco River, the second-longest in Brazil, which hosts various species of fish and has many towns on its banks.

Daily tests carried out by Brazil's national water agency ANA in the Paraopeba tributary, muddied along 200 kilometers (120 miles) by the dam burst, show the presence of metals in the water have spiked to unhealthy levels.

Residents said [...]: "Most of us here are very rural, riverside people, so we use the Paraopeba River to feed ourselves. It gives us fish, we use it to water our plants, and now we can't do this anymore, so many people have been affected by the dam breaking." [...]

The latest ANA results showed iron, magnesium and aluminum at worrying levels. [...]

Experts say the real long-term effects of the dam break at the mine, located near the town of Brumadinho and owned by Brazilian mining giant Vale, may not be evident for years. [...]

While Brumadinho is now considered Brazil's worst-ever industrial accident, given its high likely final death toll, a similar mining dam collapse three years earlier in the same region, near the town of Mariana, remains the country's worst environmental disaster. Its effects are still being measured today.

The dam near Mariana was part of a facility jointly owned by Vale. Nineteen people were killed. Pollution extended for 650 kilometers (400 miles) along a river, to the Atlantic Ocean. [...] Many residents accuse the mining giant of putting profits over lives. [...] "We are all shaken. This should never have happened. There was a lot of recklessness. Today all of Brumadinho is in mourning," said another victim. [...]

Douglas Magno/Agência France-Presse

Available at: <www.phys.org/news/2019-02-deadly-brazil-collapse-environmental-woes.html>. Accessed on: Mar. 17, 2019.

3 Read the excerpts below and write **F** (fact), **O** (opinion) or **P** (probability).

a. ◯ "Authorities fear the mineral-laced slurry released by the collapse could eventually pollute the Sao Francisco River, the second-longest in Brazil, which hosts various species of fish and has many towns on its banks."

b. ◯ "We are all shaken. This should never have happened. There was a lot of recklessness. Today all of Brumadinho is in mourning."

c. ◯ "The dam near Mariana was part of a facility jointly owned by Vale. Nineteen people were killed. Pollution extended for 650 kilometers (400 miles) along a river, to the Atlantic Ocean."

4 Now, answer the questions below in your notebook.

a. What did daily tests in the Paraopeba river indicate?

b. Before the tragedy in Brumadinho, there was another one in Mariana. What happened there?

c. In your opinion, what should mining companies and governments do to avoid such tragedies?

Text 2

5 Look at the comic strip below. What calls your attention in it? Share your impression with your classmates.

6 Look at the people in the first panel and describe their facial expression. Do they look the same in the second panel? What has changed? Write in your notebook.

7 Now read the comic strip and check the correct option.
a. The tone of the comic strip is mainly...

◯ tragic.   ◯ critical.

b. By reading the strip, we can infer that...

◯ it criticizes the way humans take care of planet Earth.

◯ it shows communication obstacles between humans and aliens.

8 Considering what you read in the text about Brumadinho, do you agree with the criticism made by the aliens? Why (not)? Share your opinion with your classmates.

Text 3

9 In 2015, artists such as Paul McCartney, Jon Bon Jovi, Sheryl Crow, Fergie, among others, got together to sing *Love song to the Earth*. What do you think is the aim of this song?

a. ◯ The song was created to call people's attention to an issue in our planet.

b. ◯ The song aims to broadcast some music festivals around the world.

10 Read the lyrics and answer the following questions in your notebook.

Love Song to the Earth

This is an open letter
From you and me together
Tomorrow's in our hands now
Find the words that matter
Say them out loud
And make it better somehow

Looking down from up on the moon
It's a tiny blue marble
Who would've thought the ground we stand on
Could be so fragile

This is a love song to the Earth
You're no ordinary world
A diamond in the universe
Heaven's poetry to us
Keep it safe, keep it safe, keep it safe
Cause it's our world, it's our world

It's not about possessions
Money, or religion
How many years we might live
When the only real question that matters
Is still a matter of perspective

Looking down from up on the moon
You're a tiny blue marble
Who would've thought the ground we stand on
Could be so fragile

This is a love song to the Earth
You're no ordinary world
Diamond in the universe
Heaven's poetry to us
Keep it safe, keep it safe, keep it safe

(Keep mother Earth safe)
Cause it's our world, it's our world

Bang Bang Bang
See Mama Earth is in a crazy mess
It's time for us to do our best
From deep sea straight up to Everest
She under crazy stress
Unless you wanna be motherless
Clean heart, green heart is the way
Is stress, speediness and too much greediness
Six billion people all want plentiness
Some people think this is harmless
(It's our world)
But if we continue there'll only be emptiness

This is a love song to the Earth
You're no ordinary world
A diamond in the universe
Heaven's poetry to us
Keep it safe, keep it safe, keep it safe
(Special paradise)
Let's keep it safe
This is a love song to the Earth
You're no ordinary world
A diamond in the universe
Heaven's poetry to us
Keep it safe, keep it safe, keep it safe

It's our world
It's our world
It's our world
It's our world
Cause it's our world

BEDINGFIELD, Natasha; GAD, Toby; McCARTNEY, Paul; SHANKS, John. Love Song to the Earth. Interpreted by: Angelique Kidjo; Colbie Caillat; Christina Grimmmie; Fergie; Johnny Rzeznik; Jon Bon Jovi; Kelsea Ballerini; Krewella; Leona Lewis; Natasha Bedingfield; Nicole Scherzinger; Paul McCartney; Q'orianka Kilcher; Sean Paul; Sheryl Crow; Victoria Justice. In: *Love Song to the Earth.*

a. What do you understand by the expression "you and me" in the verses below?

> "This is an open letter
> From you and me together"

b. Basically, a metaphor states that one thing is similar to another thing. Not literally, but by symbolism. Why do so many lyrics present metaphors?

c. The lyrics present some metaphors. Can you identify one?

d. These lyrics are organized into verses and present rhymes. Do all lyrics present the same structure?

11 Now it's up to you! In pairs, write the lyrics to a song as a tribute to our planet. Follow the
191 steps below.

a. Choose a theme that inspires you when it comes to the planet, such as the beauty of nature, forests and animals, rivers and oceans etc.

b. Write a draft of the lyrics.

c. You can use rhymes, metaphors or any other figures of speech.

d. Come up with a catchy title.

e. Don't forget that a good song is one that people can easily sing.

f. Show the draft to the teacher and make all the necessary adjustments.

g. Write the final version in the space below and present it to the class.

h. Vote for the most beautiful and creative lyrics.

TIPS FOR LIFE

Respect and preserve the environment

WAYHOME studio/Shutterstock

1 Think of one simple act you can do that could make a difference to preserve the planet.

2 In groups, create posters with green practices pictures and catchy sentences to boost sustainability. Then record a video presenting the posters.

CHECK YOUR PROGRESS	😃	😐	🙁
Environmental issues			
Conditional Sentences			
False Cognates (False Friends)			
Listening			
Speaking			
Reading			
Writing			

1 Complete the sentences with the verbs in the Present Perfect and **for** or **since**.

a. My grandparents _____ (live) in the same house _____ they got married.

b. Mr. Portillar _____ (teach) Science at this school _____ twelve years.

c. My cousin _____ (visit) over ten countries _____ 2012.

d. The eighth grade students _____ (study) French _____ the beginning of the year.

2 Complete the dialogs with the verbs in the Present Perfect or in the Simple Past.

a. **Kitty:** Hi, Carol! Sorry I couldn't call you. I _____ (be) at school since 8 a.m.

Carol: It's OK, Kitty! _____ you _____ (see) the latest Rodrigo Santoro movie?

Kitty: Yes, I _____ (see) it last night. Sally _____ (be) with me.

Carol: I _____ (love) the movie! I _____ (watch) it on Monday, after school.

Kitty: Oh, that reminds me I _____ (not buy) anything for the prom party yet.

b. **Peter:** _____ you ever _____ (be) to New Zealand?

Alice: Yes, I _____ (go) to New Zealand on my last vacation.

Peter: Polly Jones _____ (read) a lot of articles about New Zealand lately.

She _____ (ask) me to make a presentation about Australia.
Alice: I can help you. Meanwhile, what about eating something healthy?

I _____ (not eat) any junk food for two weeks.

3 Underline the correct alternative for each sentence.

a. I phoned him three days **tomorrow/ago/since**.

b. Have you **never/now/already** finished your homework?

c. Kitty has **yesterday/never/for** been to the Tijuca National Park.

d. I haven't finished the exercise **yet/just/never**.

e. My mother hasn't planted trees **since/for/just** 2018.

4 Rewrite the sentences into the active voice.

a. The Science homework will be done by Mary.

_____

b. The composition about river depollution was written by Jim.

_____

c. The Green Movement was founded by the students.

_____

d. The School Science Fair is visited by a lot of students and parents.

_____

5 Complete the ideas with the sentences below. Use the First Conditional.

the police will stop us   you will save energy

we will swim at the club   I will visit the Tijuca National Park

he will get a good mark in the Science test

a. If you turn off the air conditioning, _____.

b. If he studies a lot, _____.

c. If it isn't raining tomorrow, _____.

d. If you drive very fast, _____.

e. If I go to Rio de Janeiro, _____.

6 Complete the sentences with the First and Second Conditionals.

a. If I _____ (be) you, I _____ (not – throw) waste on the beach.

b. If you _____ (go) to bed early, you _____ (feel) better tomorrow.

c. If we _____ (be) younger, we _____ (travel) more.

d. If I _____ (be) you, I _____ (not – smoke) anymore. It's harmful!

e. Bob _____ (be) happier if Carol _____ (invite) him for the match.

f. They _____ (have) more money if they _____ (not – buy) many clothes.

g. She _____ (call) him to help us planting trees if she _____ (have) his number. But she doesn't.

UNITS 1 AND 2

1 Read the infographic below and check the correct answer.

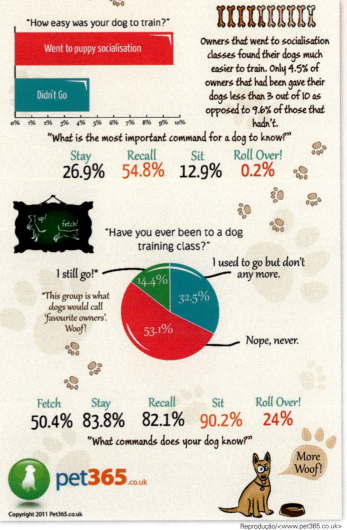

Dog Training Statistics

A well-trained dog is by far a happier dog! Why? Because a trained dog requires fewer restrictions. The more reliable the dog, the more freedom he is given. Also, he receives more attention and interaction from family members, visitors, and passers-by, than does the ill-mannered dog.

"How well-trained are they?"
My Dog vs Other Dogs

16.1% 46.2% 51.9% 23.1%

4 or 5   7 or 8
Marks out of 10 (with 10 being the best)

"Most dog owners think their dogs are better trained than those belonging to other people"

'Sit's the most well-known command with 9 out of 10 dogs knowing how to put their bums on the floor when told...

99.5% of owners think that rewarding good behaviour is most effective when training

94% of people do at least some training with their dog at home. Impressive.

Owners with 3 or more dogs were more likely to have socialised their dog when it was a puppy.
Proof that we do learn from our mistakes (eventually)!

50.6% 26.5%

Owns 3+ dogs   3 dogs or less

"Percentage of dogs socialised as puppies"

"How easy was your dog to train?"
Went to puppy socialisation
Didn't Go
0% 1% 2% 3% 4% 5% 6% 7% 8% 9% 10%

Owners that went to socialisation classes found their dogs much easier to train. Only 4.5% of owners that had been gave their dogs less than 3 out of 10 as opposed to 9.6% of those that hadn't.

"What is the most important command for a dog to know?"
Stay 26.9%   Recall 54.8%   Sit 12.9%   Roll Over! 0.2%

"Have you ever been to a dog training class?"

I still go!*   I used to go but don't any more.
14.4%   32.5%
*This group is what dogs would call 'favourite owners'. Woof!
53.1%   Nope, never.

Fetch 50.4%   Stay 83.8%   Recall 82.1%   Sit 90.2%   Roll Over! 24%
"What commands does your dog know?"

More Woof!

pet365.co.uk

Copyright 2011 Pet365.co.uk

Reprodução/<www.pet365.co.uk>

This infographic is about…

a. ◯ adoption of dogs.

b. ◯ a dogs' training survey.

c. ◯ most common pets.

2 Read the infographic again and complete the following chart.

The most known dog command	
Number of people who still go to dog training classes	
Total percentage of dogs socialised as puppies	
Command that people consider the least important	

3 Read the infographic once more and correct the statements according to the text.

a. A well-trained dog is an unhappy dog.

_____

b. A trained and reliable dog doesn't have freedom around the house.

_____

c. Ill-mannered dogs receive more attention from family members and visitors.

_____

d. Owners of one or more dogs tend to socialise their dogs when they are puppies.

_____

4 Read the infographic one more time and find synonyms for the words and expressions below.

a. to overturn: _____

b. possessor; proprietor/proprietress: _____

c. familiar, popular: _____

d. a young dog: _____

5 Answer the following questions. Then share your answers with a partner and discuss them.

a. Do you have pets? If so, do you train them?

_____

b. What command do you think is easier for a dog to learn? Why?

_____

c. Are you able to train a dog, or would you need classes to learn how to do that? Explain.

_____

_____

EXTRA PRACTICE

UNITS 3 AND 4

1 Read the blog post and choose the correct answer.

https://middleearthnj.wordpress.com/2017/10/30/benefits-of-meditation-or-mindfulness-for-youth/

Benefits of Meditation or Mindfulness for Youth

Leave a comment

October 30, 2017 by middleearthnj

Research in neuroscience has proven that meditation provides numerous benefits for children and adolescents. Benefits of meditation include:

- Reduces stress, anxiety, and even depression
- Improves grades and performance on standardized tests
- Increases attention and concentration
- Changes the brain in ways that protect against mental illness and improve control over emotions
- Increases compassion and empathy
- Improves sleep

[…]

Sirirat/Shutterstock

Role Model. If you are stressed out and never slow down, it will be very difficult to try to convince your teen that it's a good idea to act any differently. Your teen needs to see you prioritizing time each day to practice meditation and/or mindfulness. It will be an even more effective sell if you could demonstrate an ability to manage stress better as a result of these practices. Teens take seriously whatever they see in action.
[…]

Final Thoughts…
Exploring the idea of meditation with your teenager is worth the effort. Whether they like the idea of trying it or not, the truth is that meditation trains the mind to relax, focus and stay positive. It reduces anxiety, creates a sense of contentment and helps teens overcome the challenges that life throws at them. Encouraging your teen to try meditating just for five minutes a day for three weeks can help them reap the benefits and decide if the practice is right for them.

Available at: <https://middleearthnj.wordpress.com/2017/10/30/benefits-of-meditation-or-mindfulness-for-youth/>.
Accessed on: Mar. 26, 2019.

This blog post is about…

a. ◯ meditation and mindfulness school for children.

b. ◯ the rules of meditation for parents.

c. ◯ the pros of meditation for teens.

2 Read the blog post again and match the questions to the correct answers.

a. Who are the possible readers of this blog post?

b. How can parents convince their children to meditate?

c. What is one of the benefits of meditation?

d. What does neuroscience research say about meditation?

e. What happens to stress and anxiety if you meditate?

○ They can be able to manage stress better, as a result of meditation.

○ Parents and tutors.

○ They are reduced.

○ It helps teenagers to increase concentration.

○ It has proven that meditation provides numerous benefits.

3 Read the blog post once more and check **Right**, **Wrong** or **Not mentioned**.

a. Studies have shown benefits of meditation in large groups.

○ Right   ○ Wrong   ○ Not mentioned

b. Despite its various benefits, meditation does not get the sleep better.

○ Right   ○ Wrong   ○ Not mentioned

c. Parents should slow down and meditate too.

○ Right   ○ Wrong   ○ Not mentioned

d. According to research, meditation can improve performance at school.

○ Right   ○ Wrong   ○ Not mentioned

e. Teens should be encouraged to meditate for five minutes a day.

○ Right   ○ Wrong   ○ Not mentioned

4 The following words were extracted from the text. Match them to their synonyms or meanings below.

| improve | increase | slow down | effort | reap |

a. to reduce speed: _____

b. a vigorous or determined attempt: _____

c. to become better: _____

d. to make greater in size: _____

e. to receive; to obtain: _____

5 Research on mindfulness activities and share your findings with your classmates.

EXTRA PRACTICE

UNITS 5 AND 6

1 Read the article below and check the correct answer.

http://time.com/5095903/genetic-similarities-friends-study/

Friends Are More Similar Genetically Than Strangers, Study Says

BY JAMIE DUCHARME | JANUARY 12, 2018

You may have more in common with your friends than you think, according to a new study published in *Proceedings of the National Academy of Sciences.* Your genes may be similar, too.

Past research has suggested that people tend to be somewhat genetically similar to their spouses and adult friends, likely because humans naturally gravitate toward people with whom they have something in common. But how and why does this subconscious sorting happen? [...]

Overall, the researchers found that friends were more genetically similar than random pairs of people, and about two-thirds as similar as the average married couple. [...]

This effect may be due to a concept called social homophily, or the idea that individuals form bonds based on shared characteristics, many of which can be traced back to genetics.

But there may also be a second phenomenon at work, according to the paper: social structuring, or the idea that people are drawn to others in their own social environment, which may itself be partially shaped by genetics. [...]

The equation grew more interesting when the researchers compared schoolmates' genomes. Classmates were about half as genetically similar as friends and significantly more similar than unaffiliated individuals — which suggests that a shared environment and background may account for a good chunk of the genetic likeness observed among friends [...].

Available at: <http://time.com/5095903/genetic-similarities-friends-study/>. Accessed on: Apr. 2, 2019.

This article tells us about...

a. ◯ the relationship between genetics and the people in our lives.

b. ◯ genetics and our career choice.

c. ◯ how genetics increase the quality of our lives.

2 Read the article again and circle the correct option.

   a. Your genes and your friend's genes may be something you **don't have/have** in common.

   b. Adults are **genetically/strangely** similar to their spouses.

   c. People tend to be close to whom they **have something/don't have anything** in common.

   d. This effect is a kind of subconscious **sorting/genetic** modification.

   e. People form bonds based on shared **choices/characteristics**.

3 Read the article once more and match the questions to the answers.

   a. Where was the original study published?

   b. Are random pairs of people more genetically similar than friends?

   c. What is the name of the effect of genetic similarity?

   d. What is social structuring?

   e. Are classmates genetically similar?

   ◯ It is the idea that people are drawn to others in their own social environment.

   ◯ No, they aren't.

   ◯ Yes, they are.

   ◯ Homophily.

   ◯ It was part of *Proceedings of the National Academy of Sciences*.

4 The following words were extracted from the text. Read the text one more time, pay attention to the context in which these words are inserted, and match them to their meaning.

   a. research

   b. spouse

   c. sorting

   d. random

   e. unaffiliated

   f. individual

   ◯ A single person or thing.

   ◯ Not officially connected with a group.

   ◯ Systematically separate in groups according to a specific criterion.

   ◯ A husband or wife.

   ◯ Investigation and study to establish facts and reach new conclusions.

   ◯ Something chosen without method or conscious decision.

5 Do you think you are genetically similar to your classmates and friends? Discuss in small groups and share your answers with your teacher and the other classmates.

EXTRA PRACTICE

UNITS 7 AND 8

1 Read the text and check the correct answer.

Going Green as a Teen: How Youth Can Protect the Environment

As a teenager you might be wondering how you can protect the environment around you. Perhaps you enjoy sunbathing on a pristine beach on a warm summer's day… One that's free of trash, discarded food items, etc. Well there are plenty of steps you can take to ensure a better environment for today and the future. All it takes is one individual to make a difference. And just imagine the difference you and a few of your friends and family members can make. Here are a few easy ways to protect your environment.

_____
[…] Turn off lights when leaving each room and unplug items when not in use. [...] Turn computer monitors off when not in use; leaving it on with a screensaver still uses a lot of energy. Replace light bulbs with new energy-saver bulbs. Opt for rechargeable electronics instead of using batteries.

_____
Use less paper when possible… Don't doodle just to be doodling! Also, take care of your school supplies such as pens, lead pens, rulers, etc. Each one wasted means more plastic to be produced by the factories. […]

_____
Be mindful of the environment around you while enjoying days at the beach. Our beaches are beautiful and should stay that way. [...] Take a bin liner bag along with you and be sure to throw away any rubbish. […]

_____
Even as a teen, you can recycle and learn how to dump trash properly. [...]
Don't forget to recycle your mobile phones and other electronics instead of merely throwing them away. [...] If you do intend to throw it away, be sure to dispose of it properly; not doing so can harm the environment.

Available at: <https://kreolmagazine.com/travel-2/going-green-as-a-teen-how-youth-can-protect-the-environment/#. XKSbZtJKjMx>. Accessed on: Apr. 3, 2019.

The target audience of this article is…

a. ◯ parents.   **b.** ◯ young people.   **c.** ◯ teachers.

2 Read the text again and write the subheadings for each fragment. Use the suggestions from the box below.

> At the beach   At home   Recycling and dumping   At school

3 Read the text once more and answer **T** (true) or **F** (false).

a. ◯ Leaving computers on with a screensaver saves a lot of energy.

b. ◯ Using less paper at school helps to save the environment.

c. ◯ At the beach, it's important to use a bin liner bag to throw away your trash.

d. ◯ It is important to dump trash properly.

e. ◯ Do not recycle electronics. They are useless.

4 Read the text again. Then check the pictures that show good actions mentioned in the reading.

a.

Surastock/Shutterstock

b.

BaLL LunLa/Shutterstock

c.

BlurryMe/Shutterstock

d.

invisible163/Shutterstock

e.

iofoto/Shutterstock

f.

Aleksandra Suzi/Shutterstock

5 What do you already do to help save the environment? And what do you plan to do from now on? Take notes and discuss with a partner.

What I **already do** to help save the environment	What I **plan to do** to help save the environment

EXTREME SPORTS

1 Look at the image and discuss the following questions with your classmates.

a. What can you see?

b. The image shows the practice of an extreme sport. Do you know which sport it is?

c. Considering the elements you can see in the image, how do you think this sport is practiced?

Philippe Turpin/Photononstop/Getty Images

2 Read the text below and find out some information about kitesurfing. After that, give a title to the text and answer the questions.

_____

   The wind is your engine. Get ready for some huge airtime that gives you room for some incredible movements that make you forget that gravity exists. But watch out, the higher you jump the harder the landing. Without an eye for the waves and a sense for the wind it's going to cost you a lot of patience. Kitesurfers are standing on a surfboard whilst holding the kite and it takes serious power to tame the kite.

Available at: <www.extremesportscompany.com/list-of-extreme-sports>. Accessed on: Apr. 1st, 2019.

a. Does the text present any details on the practice of kitesurfing? Explain your answer.

_____

_____

b. Based on the information presented in the text, do you think kitesurfing is an easy sport to be practiced? Why (not)?

_____

_____

3 Now read a text about some curiosities on kitesurfing. Then answer the questions.

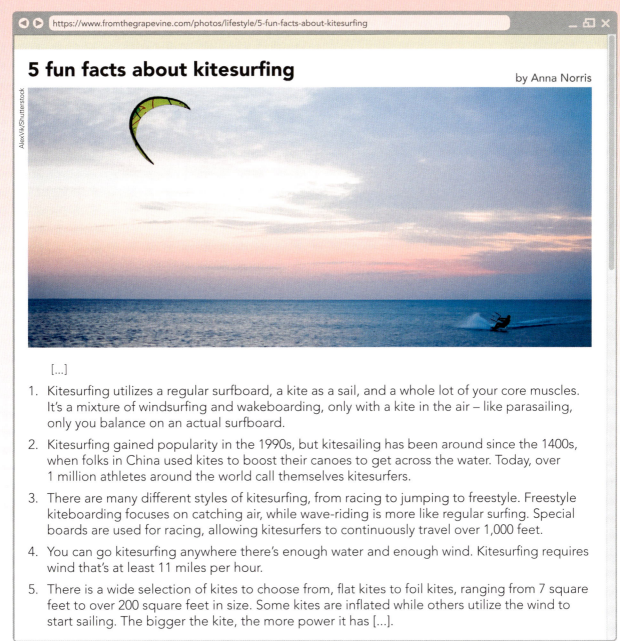

https://www.fromthegrapevine.com/photos/lifestyle/5-fun-facts-about-kitesurfing

5 fun facts about kitesurfing

by Anna Norris

[...]

1. Kitesurfing utilizes a regular surfboard, a kite as a sail, and a whole lot of your core muscles. It's a mixture of windsurfing and wakeboarding, only with a kite in the air – like parasailing, only you balance on an actual surfboard.

2. Kitesurfing gained popularity in the 1990s, but kitesailing has been around since the 1400s, when folks in China used kites to boost their canoes to get across the water. Today, over 1 million athletes around the world call themselves kitesurfers.

3. There are many different styles of kitesurfing, from racing to jumping to freestyle. Freestyle kiteboarding focuses on catching air, while wave-riding is more like regular surfing. Special boards are used for racing, allowing kitesurfers to continuously travel over 1,000 feet.

4. You can go kitesurfing anywhere there's enough water and enough wind. Kitesurfing requires wind that's at least 11 miles per hour.

5. There is a wide selection of kites to choose from, flat kites to foil kites, ranging from 7 square feet to over 200 square feet in size. Some kites are inflated while others utilize the wind to start sailing. The bigger the kite, the more power it has [...].

Available at: <www.fromthegrapevine.com/photos/lifestyle/5-fun-facts-about-kitesurfing>. Accessed on: Apr. 1st, 2019.

a. Which information presented in the text did you find more interesting? Why?

_____

_____

b. What's the main difference between this text and the text read in activity 2?

_____

_____

4 Now it's your turn to research into an extreme sport and produce a video about it. Follow the instructions your teacher is going to give you and hands on!

SAVE THE ENVIRONMENT!

◀1 Read the infographic below and answer the questions.

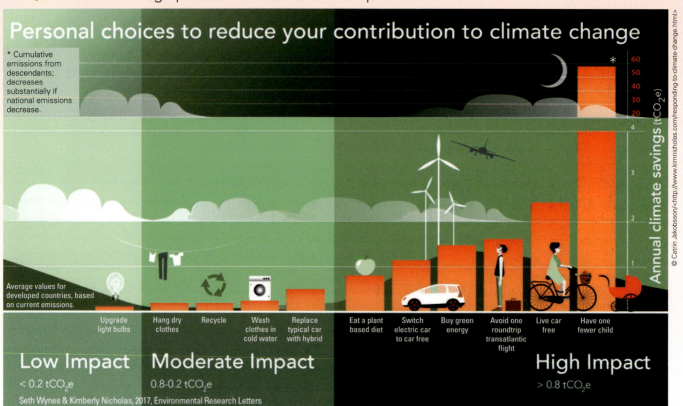

Personal choices to reduce your contribution to climate change

* Cumulative emissions from descendants; decreases substantially if national emissions decrease.

Average values for developed countries, based on current emissions.

Upgrade light bulbs | Hang dry clothes | Recycle | Wash clothes in cold water | Replace typical car with hybrid | Eat a plant based diet | Switch electric car to car free | Buy green energy | Avoid one roundtrip transatlantic flight | Live car free | Have one fewer child

Low Impact < 0.2 tCO₂e

Moderate Impact 0.8-0.2 tCO₂e

High Impact > 0.8 tCO₂e

Seth Wynes & Kimberly Nicholas, 2017, Environmental Research Letters

© Catrin Jakobsson <http://www.kimnicholas.com/responding-to-climate-change.html>

Available at: <www.phys.org/news/2017-07-effective-individual-tackle-climatediscussed.html>. Accessed on: Apr. 1th, 2019.

a. What information does the infographic above show?

_____

_____

_____

b. Considering the infographic, do you take any action in your daily routine that may contribute to the environment? If so, describe it.

_____

_____

◀2 Do you think personal choices can make a difference to the environment? Talk to your teacher and classmates about it.

_____

3 Read the following text about a teenager who takes action to make the world a better place. Then answer the questions below.

https://www.theguardian.com/world/2013/oct/18/teenagers-changing-world-malala-yousafzai

Zea Tongeman

Zea Tongeman, a 14-year-old from south London, was not a self-proclaimed tech geek. "I used to think technology was just fixing computers and saying things like: 'have you tried turning it on and off again?', like in *The IT Crowd*," she says. But when she realized, after a Little Miss Geek workshop in her school, St Saviour's and St Olave's, in Elephant and Castle, that tech could be fun and a force for good, she changed her mind. With a friend, Jordan Stirbu, she designed an app called Jazzy Recycling that aims to get people recycling by turning the sometimes tiresome task into a game.

"As Mary Poppins says: 'You find the fun and it becomes a game,' and that is exactly what our app does," she says.

Jazzy Recycling helps users find places to recycle, tells them what they can recycle and then enables them to scan, share and get rewards for their efforts.

Tapping into the teen mania for sharing even the most mundane titbits of daily life on social media, the game is then shared among friends.

Now Zea has some celebrity backing. Raj Dhonota, business consultant and an angel investor, who appeared on the Apprentice, is helping the pair build the app [...].

She says: "To have people actually using our app and to know we have made a difference would be incredible, so fingers crossed it all goes to plan."

Available at: <www.theguardian.com/world/2013/oct/18/teenagers-changing-world-malala-yousafzai>.
Accessed on: Apr. 1st, 2019.

a. What is the main objective of Zea Tongeman's creation?

_____

_____

_____

b. In your opinion, is Tongeman's app beneficial to the environment? Why (not)?

_____

_____

_____

c. Take a look at the infographic from activity 1 again. Do you think the impact of Tongeman's creation on the environment is low, moderate or high? Explain your answer.

_____

_____

_____

4 Now you are going to create an advertising campaign on saving the environment. Follow the instructions your teacher is going to give you and hands on!

FUN ACTIVITIES 1

1 Write a paragraph to continue the following detective story! Follow these steps.

- Describe what the detective was doing when Sarah called him.
- Describe how the detective was feeling at that moment, too.
- Use two or more words from the box below to create the text.
- Switch texts with a classmate and find out how he/she continued his/her story.

Ilustrações: Filipe Rocha/ Arquivo da editora

| surprised | frightened | alert | interested | cold | angry | sleepy |

The sun was rising in the sky. Sarah, a 72-year-old woman, got up and was shocked when she realized that her expensive wedding ring had been stolen while she was sleeping. She had no doubt about what to do. She called her old friend, detective Phillip.

_____

_____

2 Unscramble the letters to form words and complete the crossword puzzle with the names of extreme sports.

1. praruok
2. tanigrf
3. aykaingk
4. nrfisgu
5. limbgnic
6. rrvei ncosirsg

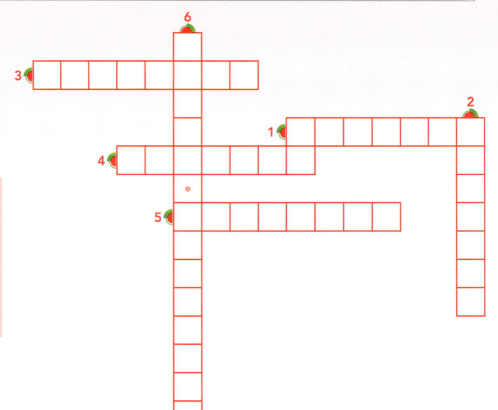

3   Match the columns to make sentences about your life. Write new phrases in the blank spaces. Then talk to a classmate about your answers.

a. I must
b. I should
c. I don't need to

- ○ play less video game.
- ○ check my smartphone less often.
- ○ spend more time with my friends.
- ○ visit more cultural sites.
- ○ read and study more.
- ○ be in contact with nature.
- ○
- ○

4   Use the words from the box to label the following types of exercises available at the gym. There are two extra words in the box.

dumbbell weight   treadmill   stretching   jumping rope

exercise bike   push-up   sit-up

Filipe Rocha/Arquivo da editora

FUN ACTIVITIES 2

1 Why do these brothers look so different? Unscramble the letters to form words to complete the statements. Then write **T** (true) or **F** (false).

○ Because they don't have the same

_____ (segen).

○ Because the _____ (nenvorimten) in which they grew up was not the same.

○ Because, as _____ (enGetcis) states, the way they lived didn't influence their personality.

2 What are the feelings related to positive and negative peer pressure? Organize the words from the box into two lists as indicated below. Then reflect on the subject and complete the lists with other feelings. Use a dictionary.

| confident | glad | frustrated | unhappy | bored | anxious | confused |
| insecure | hopeful | guilty | shocked | embarrassed |

Ilustrações: Filipe Rocha/Arquivo da editora

_____   _____

_____   _____

_____   _____

_____   _____

_____   _____

3 Read the definitions below and complete the crossword puzzle. Number one is already done for you.

1. A sudden violent movement of the Earth's surface, often causing damage.
2. To become covered with water.
3. The state of the body not having enough food.
4. A strong, dangerous wind that forms itself into an upside-down spinning cone.
5. Damage caused to water, air, etc. by harmful substances or waste.
6. A long period when there is little or no rain and people do not have enough water.

Based on: <https://dictionary.cambridge.org/pt/>.
Accessed on: Apr. 1, 2019.

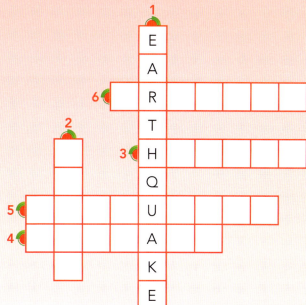

4 Match the human actions to their consequences to the enviroment.

a. Plant trees.

b. Turn off the lights when nobody is using it.

c. No littering.

d. Recycle cardboard, plastic, and household waste.

e. Walk, ride or cycle to school.

◯ Reduction of CO_2 emissions.

◯ Release more oxygen into the atmosphere.

◯ Cleaner streets and public places.

◯ Energy saving.

◯ Reduction of pollution caused by recyclabe waste.

GLOSSARY

A

accomplish: alcançar; atingir
accurate: exato/a, preciso/a
ache: dor
actual: real, verdadeiro
addict: viciado/a
adulthood: idade adulta
advertisement: anúncio
affect: afetar
aging: envelhecimento
agreement: acordo
aim: aspirar, almejar
alignment: alinhamento
alive: vivo/a
alongside: junto (a)
already: já
amid: entre, no meio de
amusement park: parque de diversões
ancient: antigo/a
anger: enraivecer-se; raiva
announcement: aviso, anúncio
annoyed: aborrecido/a
antler: chifre; galhada
anxious: ansioso/a
anywhere: qualquer lugar
apart: separado/a
ape: símio; macaco
apologize: desculpar-se
appearance: aparência
argue: discutir; brigar
assertiveness: precisão; confiança
at least: pelo menos
attempting: tentar; tentativa
audience: público, plateia
automated: automatizado/a
aware: ciente, a par
awful: horrível

B

baboon: babuíno
baby boomer: geração que fez parte de uma explosão demográfica dos anos 1960
background: experiência acumulada
backpain: dor nas costas
bad: mau; ruim
barbell: barra para levantamento de peso
bark: casca de árvore; latir
bass: grave (som); baixo (instrumento musical)
beauty: beleza
bed net: mosquiteiro
bee: abelha
behavior: comportamento
being: ser, criatura
bend: dobrar-se, curvar-se
betray: trair
bill: conta, fatura
bit: pouco/a
boast: ostentar
bored: entediado/a
boss: chefe; dar ordens para, mandar em
bother: incomodar
boundary: fronteira; limite
brain: cérebro
brake: frear; parar
brave: valente
breeding: reprodução; procriação
bridge: ponte
briefly: brevemente
broadcast: transmitir; difundir; divulgar
browse: navegar pela internet
bucket list: lista das coisas para fazer antes de morrer
bug: defeito; inseto
build: construir
building: construção; edifício
bullet: bala, munição
bungee jumping: salto com elástico
bunny: coelhinho/a
burn: queimar
burst: irromper; invadir; romper

C

canvas: tela; lona
careless: descuidado/a; desleixado/a, indiferente
carpool: carona solidária
carriers: carregadores/as
carry out: realizar; fazer
cart: carrinho (de compras)
caught: pego/a
cave: caverna
ceiling: teto
century: século
certain: certo/a; seguro/a
chat: conversar; bater papo
checkup: exame médico completo
cheer up: animar-se, alegrar-se
cheerful: animado/a; alegre
chest: peito, tórax
chew: mascar, mastigar
chigger: bicho-de-pé
chugging away: trabalhando sem parar
chunk: parte
citizen: cidadão/cidadã
climbing: escalada, alpinismo
close: fechar; perto, próximo/a
clothes: roupas
cloudy: nublado
coaching: treinamento
coastal: costeiro/a
come back: voltar
come true: virar realidade
comic strip: tirinha; quadrinhos
compelling: convincente; atraente
compostables: composteiras
compound: composto/a
conceive: conceber
concern: preocupação; interesse
contest: competição
convey: transmitir
cottage: chalé, cabana
couch potato: pessoa sedentária
counterparts: colegas
countless: incontável
couple: casal, par
cover: capa
co-worker: colega de trabalho
cramp: cãibra
crease: marca; vinco
crop: plantação
cross-legged: de pernas cruzadas
crowded: lotado/a
crown: coroa
crumble: desintegrar-se
crush: arrasar
crust: casca; crosta
crystal-clear: cristalino/a; transparente
cub: filhote (de urso, leão)
cues: sugestões
curse: praguejar

cyberbullying: assédio digital
cypress: cipreste

D

dam: barragem; represa
danger: perigo
dangerous: perigoso/a
dare: ousar
daredevil: intrépido/a; audacioso/a
darkness: escuridão
dash over: deslizar
date: data; namorar
dead: morto/a
deadline: prazo final
deadly: mortal
deaf: surdo/a
deal: lidar, tratar; acordo
death tool: número de mortos
debris: destroços
deed: ação; feito
deep: profundo/a
deer: veado, cervo
dental floss: fio dental
deploying: implantado/a
deprivation: privação; carência
devoted: devotado/a
die: morrer
differ: diferir, ser diferente
dip: mergulho
disgust: enojar, repugnar
disorder: distúrbio
displaced: deslocado/a
disposable: descartável
distort: distorcer
diver: mergulhador/a
diving: mergulho
double: dobrar; duplo; dobro
down: abaixo; para baixo
downhill: morro abaixo
downright: completo/a
drag: arrastar
drier: secador/a
driving crazy: deixar louco/a; enlouquecer alguém
drop: descer; cair
drought: seca
drug: droga
dude: cara; sujeito
dumbbell weight: haltere
dusty: empoeirado/a

E

earn: ganhar por seu trabalho ou esforço
Earth: planeta Terra
earthquake: terremoto
effort: esforço
elderly: idoso/a
elude: escapar
embarrassed: envergonhado/a
employment: emprego, trabalho
empty: vazio/a
endurance: resistência
enhance: acentuar; destacar
ensure: assegurar
entertained: entretido/a
entrepreneur: empreendedor/a
envy: inveja
even: mesmo, até mesmo
even though: apesar de que, embora
evil: mal
evolve: evoluir
exploitation: exploração
extreme sport: esporte radical
eyebrow: sobrancelha

F

fail: falhar
fairly: razoavelmente
faith: fé
fall in love: apaixonar-se
farming: agricultura, lavoura
farther: mais distante, mais longe
fault: culpa
fear: medo; temer
fearless: destemido/a
feed: alimentar
feeling: sentimento
fetus: feto
fewer: menos
figure: algarismo; figura
fill up: encher
finger: dedo (da mão)
fingerspelling: datilologia, alfabeto manual
fire: fogo
firefighter: bombeiro/a
fish: peixe
fitness: condicionamento físico
fix: consertar
flash: clarão breve e intenso
flat: plano/a, achatado/a
flaunt: ostentar
flea: pulga
flesh: carne; polpa de fruta
flex: flexionar
flight: voo
flip: virada
float: flutuar

flood: inundação, enchente
flour: farinha
flow: fluir; circular; fluxo
fly: voar; mosca
fool: tolo/a, bobo/a
foothill: base da montanha
footprint: pegada
forecast: previsão
forerunner: precursor
forever: para sempre
foreword: introdução
forgive: perdoar
fortunately: felizmente
fortune teller: vidente
forward: para a frente, adiante
foul: repugnante
fragile: frágil
free-climber: montanhista; escalador/a
freezing: gelado/a, congelado/a
freshwater: de água doce
frightened: assustado/a
fringed: cercado/a, margeado/a
from scratch: do início, do começo
fuel: combustível
fur: pelo de animal
further: mais distante; além; além disso

G

garbage: lixo
gardening: jardinagem
garnered: reuniu
gear: engrenagem; acessórios, equipamento
get away with: sair impune; safar-se
gift: dom; presente
give rise to: dar origem a
give up: desistir
glacier: geleira
glasses: óculos
glide: deslizar
global warming: aquecimento global
gloves: luvas
goat: cabra
googles: óculos de natação
gorgeous: magnífico/a, maravilhoso/a
gossip: fofoca
grab: pegar; agarrar
greediness: mesquinhez
greener: pessoas que têm atitudes de proteção ao meio ambiente
grip: ação de agarrar, segurar, aperto
groom: arrumar-se
ground: chão
grow old: envelhecer
guilt: culpa
gum: goma de mascar, chiclete

H

hailed: aclamado/a
half: metade; meio/a
handbag: bolsa
handshaking: aperto de mãos
hang: pendurar
hang gliding: voo de asa-delta
hang out: passar o tempo em um lugar com alguém
hang up: desligar abruptamente
harass: assediar; molestar
hare: lebre
harm: causar dano, danificar
harness: aproveitar
haunt: perseguir
headache: dor de cabeça
headline: título; manchete
healing: cura
hearing-aid: aparelho auditivo
heightened: elevado/a; intensificado/a
held: realizado/a
hide: esconder; ocultar
higher: superior
highlighted: destacado/a
hill: morro
hole: buraco
honor: homenagear
hopeful: esperançoso/a
hopeless: desesperançado/a, desesperado/a
housework: serviço doméstico
how long: quanto tempo
hunger: fome
hurtful: doloroso/a; prejudicial

I

ice cream: sorvete
icy: gelado/a
illness: doença
in a flash: em um instante
in spite of: apesar de
indeed: na verdade; certamente; de fato
indoor: interno/a, de dentro de casa
infamous: má fama; infame
inherit: herdar
injury: ferimento; lesão
interview: entrevista
interviewer: entrevistador/a
into: para dentro de
intricately: intrinsecamente; profundamente
inwardly: por dentro
issue: assunto, questão

J

jar: pote, frasco
jealous: ciumento/a; invejoso/a
jelly: geleia; gelatina
join: juntar-se
joke: piada
jolt: choque
jump over: pular por cima
jumping jack: polichinelo
jungle: selva
junk food: comida calórica e pouco nutritiva

K

keen: afiado/a
keep track: estar informado/a
kick: chutar
kidding: brincando; fazendo piada
killed: morto/a
kitchen: cozinha
knee: joelho
knock: bater
know: saber; conhecer
knowledge: conhecimento

L

lab: laboratório
lack of: falta de
lamb: cordeiro
landing: pouso
landscape: paisagem, cenário
lately: ultimamente
later: posterior; mais tarde
laughter: risada
lay: botar
lay down: deitar-se
lazy: preguiçoso/a
leap: saltar; pular
learning: aprendizagem; conhecimento
least: menos
leave: deixar; sair; folhas
lecture: palestra
leek: alho-poró
legible: legível
legs: pernas
leisurely: lento/a; lentamente
lend: emprestar
life-giving: revigorante
lift: levantar; elevador (inglês britânico)
lighting: iluminação
link: ligação
lip: lábio
lip-reading: leitura labial
literacy: alfabetização
lobby: encorajar, persuadir, convencer

loft: sótão
lonely: solitário/a, isolado/a
look away: ignorar
look forward: aguardar ansiosamente
loudly: ruidosamente
lower back: região lombar
luckily: por sorte
lush: exuberante
lynx: lince

mad: maluco/a
mail: enviar pelo correio
make sure: certificar-se de, assegurar-se de
malaise: mal-estar
maneuver: manobra
mankind: humanidade
marriage: casamento
marry: casar
massive: maciço/a
mate: colega
matter: problema; questão; importar
mature: maduro/a
mayor: prefeito/a
meaning: significado
meanwhile: enquanto isso
measured: medido/a
meat: carne
meatball: almôndega
meeting: reunião
melt: derreter
mess: bagunça; confusão
mice: ratos
mirror: espelho
miss: sentir falta de; perder
misuse: abuso; mau uso
mock: zombar
mockingbird: pássaro tordo-dos-remédios
monk: monge
mood: humor; disposição
moon: lua
morph into: transformar-se em
mourning: luto; lamento
mouth: boca
move away: afastar
moviegoers: frequentador/a de cinema
moving: comovente
mud: lama
muffin: bolinho doce
mumble: resmungar; murmurar
murdered: assassinado/a

napkin: guardanapo
nearly: quase; aproximadamente
needle: agulha
neighbor: vizinho/a

neighborhood: bairro, vizinhança
neither: nenhum; nem
new: novo/a
newborn: recém-nascido/a
nightmare: pesadelo
no one: ninguém
nobody: ninguém
nod: aprovar, assentir com a cabeça
noise: barulho
nonetheless: apesar de tudo
non-profit: que não visa a lucro
notice: aviso; notar, reparar
novel: romance (livro)
nowhere: em lugar nenhum
nun: freira
nurse: enfermeiro/a

obey: obedecer
occur: ocorrer
odds: probabilidades, chances
office: escritório
offspring: prole; filhos
old-fashioned: ultrapassado/a
once: uma vez
ongoing: em curso
onset: início
order: ordem; pedido
outbreak: surto
outdoor: parte externa
outnumber: exceder em número; extrapolar
overall: total; geral
overestimate: superestimar
overflow: transbordar
overweight: sobrepeso
owe: dever algo a alguém
owner: proprietário/a

pace: passo; ritmo
paired: emparelhado/a
pampered: paparicado/a
panel: placa; painel
pants: calças
part-time: meio expediente
pattern: padrão
paws: patas
peak: pico
pea: ervilha
pear: pera
peek: espiar
peer: colega
peer pressure: pressão dos colegas
peppered: salpicado/a
pin up: prender
pious: piedoso/a

pivotal: crucial
plague: peste, epidemia
playful: brincalhão/brincalhona
pleasant: agradável
pledge: adesão
point: apontar; ponto
poverty: pobreza
power: força
power walking: caminhada em ritmo acelerado
praise: elogiar; elogio
pray: rezar
predict: prevê
pregnancy: gravidez
prejudice: preconceito
pretend: fingir
preview: pré-estreia; amostra
profit: lucro
prom: baile de formatura
proper: apropriado/a
proud: orgulhoso/a
psychic: paranormal
pull: puxar
push: empurrar
push-ups: flexões de braço
puzzled: confuso/a

quiet: tranquilo/a, silencioso/a
quit: parar de, deixar de
quite: bem; completamente

rack: cabide
rainforest: floresta tropical
rampant: desenfreado/a
rash: erupção cutânea; irritação
realize: perceber, dar-se conta
rechargeable: recarregável
recipient: destinatário/a
recklessness: negligência
recover: recuperar-se, restabelecer-se
refrain: abster-se, refrear, conter
regret: arrepender-se
release: lançar
relieve: aliviar; acalmar
rely on: depender de alguém/algo, contar com alguém/algo
remaining: restante
remind: lembrar alguém de (fazer) algo
require: exigir
researcher: pesquisador/a
retreat: retiro; refúgio
review: resenha; crítica
reward: recompensa, prêmio
rights: direitos

rim: borda
rise: levantar-se; originar-se; subir
risk: risco
risktaker: pessoa que corre riscos
riverbank: margem de rio
role: papel
route: trajeto
rubber: borracha
rubber tapper: seringueiro/a
rush: correr; apressar-se; precipitar-se

safe: seguro/a
save: salvar; poupar
scavenger hunt: caça ao tesouro
scenic: pitoresco/a; aprazível
scent: odor
scoop: bola, colher; furo jornalístico
scouring: esquadrinhando
screenshot: captura de tela
scuba: cilindro (para mergulho)
scuba diving: mergulho com tanque de oxigênio
seat: assento; lugar
seek: procurar
seem: parecer
seizure: convulsão
self-confidence: autoconfiança
selfish: egoísta
self-respect: amor-próprio
servings: porções
set out: pôr-se a caminho, sair, partir
setbacks: contratempos
several: vários/as
sew: costurar
sewer: esgoto
shadow: sombra
shame: vergonha
share: compartilhar
sharp: precisão; em ponto
sheep: ovelha
shelter: abrigo; proteção
shine: brilhar
ship: navio
shipwreck: naufragar; naufrágio
shirt: camisa
shivering: tremendo
shoes: sapatos
shoot off: disparar
shortage: escassez; falta
shot: tiro
shoulder: ombro
shout: gritar; grito
shower: chuveiro; tomar banho (de chuveiro)
shrinking violet: mosca-morta
shy: tímido/a

sick: doente, enjoado/a
side: lado
sidewalk: calçada
sit-ups: abdominais
size: tamanho
skater: patinador/a; esqueitista
sketches: rascunhos
skiing: esqui
skill: habilidade
skin: pele
skip: evitar; pular; perder de propósito
skunk: gambá
skydiving: paraquedismo
sleeping bag: saco de dormir
sleepover: dormir na casa de um/a amigo/a
sleeve: manga (de roupa)
slicker: capa impermeável
slide: escorregar
slipper: chinelo
slow down: abrandar; retardar; desacelerar
slowly: lentamente
small: pequeno/a
smallpox: varíola
smart: esperto/a, inteligente
smelly: malcheiroso/a
smoke: fumaça; fumar
snack: lanche
snowy: coberto de neve
soaring: disparando; aumentando
social butterfly: pessoa muito sociável; arroz de festa
soil: solo
solve: resolver
somebody: alguém
someone: alguém
somewhere: algum lugar
son: filho
sore: dolorido/a
sort: espécie, tipo
soul: alma
southeast: sudoeste
southern: do sul
speak up: falar o que pensa; manifestar-se
speaker: alto-falante
speech: discurso
speech bubble: balão de diálogo
speediness: rapidez
spelling: soletrar
spin: girar; giro
spoilt (spoiled): mimado/a
spotlight: destaque
spread: espalhar
spring: primavera
squeak: chiado; chiar, ranger
squeal: grunhir, chiar
squid: lula
staff: pessoal, quadro de funcionários
standing water: água parada

stare: olhar fixamente
statement: declaração; sentença
statewide: estadual
steadily: regular; constante
steak: bife
steal: roubar
steep: íngreme
steer: virar o volante, fazer curva
stem: caule, haste
stem cell: célula-tronco
step: passo
storage: armazenagem
storm: temporal
strain: pressão; tensão
strap: amarrar, segurar
straw: canudo
street ludge: descida em trenó de rua
strength: força
strengthen: fortalecer
stretch: esticar
stretching: alongamento
strewn: coberto/a
striking: impressionante
strip off: despir-se
struck: atingiu
struggle: luta
stuck: preso/a
stun: chocar, aturdir
stunning: maravilhoso/a; estonteante
stunt: manobra; acrobacia
successful: bem-sucedido/a
sum up: resumir
summer: verão
sunny: ensolarado/a
sunshine: luz do Sol
surface: superfície
surgeon: cirurgião/ã
survive: sobreviver
survivor: sobrevivente
sustainability: sustentabilidade
sustainable: sustentável
swallow: engolir
sweetheart: querido/a
swimmer: nadador/a
swore: xingou

tag: etiqueta; marcar
tame: domar
tan: bronzeado
teamwork: trabalho em grupo
tease: provocar, mexer com
tender: macio/a; terno/a
tent: barraca
terrain: terreno
terrific: ótimo/a, estupendo/a
thousands: milhares
thrill: emoção, vibração
thumbs: polegares
thus: assim

thwarted: frustrado/a; impedido/a
tick: carrapato
tick off: riscar; desmarcar
till: até; até que
times: vezes
tiny: minúsculo/a
tire: pneu
tissue: tecido
toad: sapo
toll-free: gratuidade
tone: timbre; tom (de voz)
tool: ferramenta
tossed salad: salada mista
touching: comovente
towards: para (em direção a)
track: seguir, procurar; trilha
track suit: agasalho; roupa desportiva
trademark: marca registrada
trail: trilha
trainer: treinador/a
trait: traço, característica
traverse: atravessar
treadmill: esteira
trend: tendência
trick: truque
triggered: desencadeou; desencadeado/a
troublemarker: agitador/a; encrenqueiro/a
trumpet: trompete
trunk: tronco
trust: confiar; confiança
trustworthy: confiável
tumble: derrubar
turmoil: distúrbio, desordem
twice: duas vezes
type: tipo
typewriter: máquina de escrever

ultimately: por fim, finalmente
umbrella: guarda-chuva
unbelievable: inacreditável
uncomfortable: desconfortável
undergoing: passando por
undoubtedly: indubitavelmente, sem dúvida
unemployment: desemprego
unlike: ao contrário de
unpleasant: desagradável
unraveled: desvendado/a
untouched: intocado/a
upbeat: para cima; animado/a
upload: carregar
upper: elevado/a; mais alto/a
upset: abalado/a

upward slant: inclinação ascendente
user: usuário/a
ushering: apontando o caminho para alguém

venue: local de encontro
vowel: vogal

waiter: garçom
warm: quente
warm up: aquecimento
warn: avisar, prevenir; alertar
warning: aviso
wash: lavar
waste: desperdiçar
waterskiing: esqui aquático
wave: onda
weather: tempo, clima
West: Ocidente
wheat: trigo
wheel: roda
whether: se
whirlybird: helicóptero (inglês norte-americano arcaico)
white lie: mentira inofensiva
widely: amplamente
wife: esposa
wildfire: incêndio fora de controle em floresta
wildlife: vida selvagem
willingly: de boa vontade
wind: vento
wise: sábio/a
without: sem
woe: desgraça
women: mulheres
wonder: perguntar-se; admirar-se
work out: exercitar-se
workout: exercício físico
worldwide: mundial, por todo o mundo
worried: preocupado/a
worry: preocupar-se

yellow fever: febre amarela
yet: ainda
yield: rendimento
youth: juventude

zorbing: atividade em que alguém desce uma colina ou fluxo de água em uma grande bola de plástico transparente

IRREGULAR VERBS

Os verbos podem assumir sentidos diferentes dos listados abaixo, portanto é preciso atentar ao contexto para compreender o significado e o uso de cada um deles.

Base Form	Simple Past	Past Participle	Translation
be	was/were	been	ser; estar
become	became	become	tornar-se
break	broke	broken	quebrar
bring	brought	brought	trazer
buy	bought	bought	comprar
choose	chose	chosen	escolher
come	came	come	vir
do	did	done	fazer
eat	ate	eaten	comer
fall	fell	fallen	cair
feel	felt	felt	sentir(-se)
find	found	found	encontrar, descobrir
get	got	got/gotten	obter; conseguir; pegar
give	gave	given	dar
go	went	gone	ir
grow	grew	grown	crescer; cultivar
have	had	had	ter
hear	heard	heard	ouvir
know	knew	known	saber; conhecer
lead	led	led	levar; conduzir
learn	learnt/learned	learnt/learned	aprender
lose	lost	lost	perder
make	made	made	fazer
meet	met	met	encontrar
read	read	read	ler
say	said	said	dizer
see	saw	seen	ver
send	sent	sent	mandar, enviar
speak	spoke	spoken	falar
spend	spent	spent	gastar; passar tempo
teach	taught	taught	ensinar
tell	told	told	dizer a, contar
think	thought	thought	pensar
wake	woke/waked	woken/waked	acordar
win	won	won	vencer; ganhar
write	wrote	written	escrever

GRAMMAR HELPER

UNIT 1

Simple Present, Simple Past and Simple Future

O *Simple Present* é usado para expressar ações rotineiras ou habituais no presente.

Affirmative	My neighbor **listens** to music every morning.
Interrogative	**Do** you **go** to school by bus every day?
Negative	I **don't watch** TV because I prefer to watch videos online.

O *Simple Past* é usado para ações que tiveram início e foram concluídas no passado.

Affirmative	My neighbor **listened** to music last night.
Interrogative	**Did** you **go** to school by bus yesterday?
Negative	I **didn't watch** TV last weekend.

O *Simple Future* é usado para falar de ações futuras e fazer previsões.

Affirmative	My neighbor **will listen** to music today.
Interrogative	**Will** you **go** to school by bus tomorrow?
Negative	I **won't watch** TV tonight because I need to do my homework.

◀1 Complete the sentences with the Simple Present, Simple Past or Simple Future of the verbs in parentheses.

a. Will it rain? It _____ tomorrow. (be – negative)

b. This remote control _____ because the battery is old. (work – negative)

c. _____ you _____ fun at the party last night? Yes, I did! It was a great party! (have – interrogative)

d. Chris _____ his favorite TV show today because he

_____ his homework last night. He _____ to do it right now. (watch – negative/do – negative/need – affirmative)

Present Continuous and Past Continuous

O *Present Continuous* é usado para descrever uma ação que está ocorrendo no momento da fala.

Affirmative	She **is** read**ing** a very interesting biography.
Interrogative	**Is** she read**ing** a very interesting biography?
Negative	She **isn't** read**ing** a very interesting biography.

O *Past Continuous* é usado para descrever uma ação em andamento no passado.

Affirmative	She **was** read**ing** a very interesting biography.
Interrogative	**Was** she read**ing** a very interesting biography?
Negative	She **wasn't** read**ing** a very interesting biography.

2 Complete the sentences with the Present Continuous or the Past Continuous. Use the verbs in parentheses.

a. The baby _____ while the TV was on. (play – affirmative)

b. What a beautiful morning! The sun _____ and the sky is clear! (shine – affirmative)

c. Lindsay _____ to a word you _____ because she was distracted. (listen – negative/say – affirmative)

d. I'm not busy now, I _____ to music. (listen – affirmative)

Future with Going to

O *Future with Going to* é usado para descrever ações planejadas ou intenções no futuro.

Affirmative	My parents **are going to** cook dinner tonight.
Interrogative	**Are** my parents **going to** cook dinner tonight?
Negative	My parents **aren't going to** cook dinner tonight.

3 Complete the sentences with **going to** and the verbs in parentheses.

a. The store _____ in ten minutes, we need to hurry up! (close – affirmative)

b. _____ you _____ that last slice of pizza? (eat – interrogative)

c. I have a feeling this plan of yours _____. (work – negative)

d. What _____ you _____ today?

I _____ my laundry. (do – interrogative/affirmative)

Some, Any and No

As palavras *some*, *any* e *no* expressam quantidade. É possível usá-las ou usar palavras delas derivadas para se referir a pessoas, coisas e lugares. *Some* e *no* podem ser usadas em frases afirmativas (note que, apesar de *no* ser uma expressão negativa, ela é usada em frases afirmativas) e *any*, em frases negativas e interrogativas.

Compound Words	
People	somebody/someone, anybody/anyone, nobody/no one
Things	something, anything, nothing
Places	somewhere, anywhere, nowhere

4 Complete with **some**, **any**, **no** or their compound words.

a. Are there _____ tickets left for the Lady Gaga concert?

b. There is _____ in the classroom this morning. It is empty!

c. Where is Lisa? She has to be _____ near here.

d. There is _____ wrong with my computer. It doesn't start!

UNIT 2

Modal Verbs

Os *modal verbs* são verbos auxiliares que complementam o significado do verbo principal.

Modal	Usage	Example
Can	Permission (informal)	**Can** I go to the restroom, please?
	Request (informal)	**Can** you help me prepare lunch today?
	Ability	I **can** ride a bicycle. **Can** you ride one, too?
	Possibility	I **can** help you if you want me to.
May	Permission (formal)	**May** we start our meeting now?
	Possibility (formal)	You **may** be tired after the marathon.
Might	Possibility (formal)	You **might** want to order your food now.
Could	Request (informal)	**Could** you give this book back to the teacher, please?
	Possibility (formal)	The principal **could** send us the report cards.
	Ability (past)	**Could** you ride a bike when you were 6 years old?
Would	Offer	**Would** you like something to drink?
	Invitation	**Would** you like to come to my house tomorrow?

1 Circle the correct modal verb to complete each sentence.

   a. I **wouldn't/can't** skateboard yet, but I'm having some lessons.

   b. **Would/Could** you count up to ten in English when you were 5 years old?

   c. Teacher, **can't/may** I come in? Sorry, I'm late this morning.

   d. **Might/Would** you like to have chicken or fish for dinner tonight?

Tag Questions

As *tag questions* são usadas em final de frase para confirmar a informação que foi dada. Se a sentença estiver na forma **afirmativa**, a *tag question* deve ficar na forma **negativa**. Se a sentença estiver na forma **negativa**, a *tag question* deve ficar na forma **afirmativa**.

I'**m not** going to pass this test, **am** I?

The mailman **didn't** arrive yet, **did** he?

We **will** travel to Orlando on our next vacation, **won't** we?

2 Fill in the gaps with the correct tag questions.

   a. We will come back from Toronto as soon as possible, _____?

   b. Paul, you didn't do the dishes, _____?

   c. Carlos doesn't like chocolate cake, _____?

   d. The dog was playing in the backyard, _____?

UNIT 3

Subject Pronouns, Possessive Adjectives and Possessive Pronouns

Subject Pronouns	Possessive Adjectives	Possessive Pronouns
(usados como sujeitos de uma oração)	(usados para indicar posse; são acompanhados de substantivo)	(usados para indicar posse; não são acompanhados de substantivo)
I	my	mine
you	your	yours
he	his	his
she	her	hers
it	its	–
we	our	ours
you	your	yours
they	their	theirs

1 Underline the correct word to complete each sentence.

   a. What about this school objects? Are they **she/theirs/my**?

   b. Whose phone number is that? I think it is **her/we/yours**.

   c. What color is your pencil case, Melinda? **Mine/I/My** is gray and green.

   d. **Ours/He/We** don't have any Math homework for tomorrow.

Modal Verbs

Como estudado na unidade 2, os *modal verbs* são verbos auxiliares que complementam o significado do verbo principal.

Modal	Usage	Example
Should	Give advice; make a recommendation	You **should** respect other cultures.
Must	Obligation	You **must** do the test with a blue pen.
Mustn't	Prohibition	We **mustn't** talk during the movie.

2 Complete the sentences below using the correct modal verb. The cues in parentheses may help you.

   a. Alicia _____ get a haircut. Her hair is really long now. (advice)

   b. Travelers _____ take any artifacts from this historical site. (prohibition)

   c. Maybe you _____ start taking private Spanish lessons. (advice)

   d. You _____ return these books to the library today! (obligation)

UNIT 4

Relative Clauses and Relative Pronouns

A *relative clause* é uma oração que não existe sozinha: ela depende de uma oração principal, e sua função é trazer informação sobre um substantivo ou pronome citado nessa oração. Para retomar esse antecedente e conectar as duas orações, são usados os *relative pronouns*.

Relative Pronoun	Usage	Example
Who/That	They are used to refer to people.	People eat more fruit and vegetables. They are healthier. People **who/that** eat more fruit and vegetables are healthier.
Which/That	They are used to refer to things.	The video clip showed the new song. It was exciting. The video clip **which/that** showed the new song was exciting.
Whose	It is used to indicate possession.	Machado de Assis was born in Rio de Janeiro. His first name was Joaquim. Machado de Assis, **whose** first name was Joaquim, was born in Rio de Janeiro.

◀1 Complete the sentences with the correct Relative Pronoun.

    a. The girl, _____ father is a famous actor, is a new student in my school.

    b. The computer program _____ the teacher is using is brand new.

    c. That couple _____ is looking for their dog looks really sad.

    d. The student _____ arrived late in class was Joseph.

Used to

A estrutura *used to* é utilizada para expressar hábito, ação ou estado recorrentes no passado, que já não acontecem mais no presente.

1. Na forma afirmativa, utiliza-se a estrutura: sujeito + *used to* + verbo principal.

    I **used to sleep** really early when I was a child.

2. Na forma negativa, é usada a estrutura: sujeito + *didn't use to* + verbo principal.

    I **didn't use to study** hard, but now I have to do so.

3. Na forma interrogativa, é usada a estrutura: *did* + sujeito + *use to* + verbo principal.

    Did you **use to play** with dolls when you were a baby?

◀2 Complete the sentences with **used to** and the verbs in parentheses.

    a. I _____ studying Math, but now I like it! (hate)

    b. My mother _____ French when she was younger, but she can't remember most of it. (study)

    c. My family _____ in Japan, but we moved to São Paulo last year. (live)

    d. I _____ videogames when I was younger, I preferred playing with wooden toys. (play)

UNIT 5

Linking words

As *linking words* são palavras utilizadas para conectar ideias e informações em uma frase.

Sandra **and** her daughter want to take a vacation, **but** they don't have money.

The teacher is not coming today **because** she is sick. **So**, students will send her flowers.

Addition	Consequence	Contrast	Condition
in addition, and, also, as well as	consequently, thus, as a result, so	but, however	as long as, if
Conclusion	**Reason**	**Time**	**Emphasis**
in conclusion, summing up, finally	because, as, since	first, then, secondly, before, after	for sure, indeed, absolutely, clearly, undoubtedly

◀1 Check the linking words that complete the sentences appropriately.

a. Mary is finishing her test, _____ she can't leave the classroom yet.
   ◯ so   ◯ but

b. Julie is a very good student. She is _____ a nice person.
   ◯ also   ◯ however

c. John is a good student, _____ he can't get a good grade in Math.
   ◯ thus   ◯ but

UNIT 6
Present Perfect

O *Present Perfect* é um tempo verbal que expressa ações iniciadas no passado e que ainda estão ocorrendo ou repercutindo no presente.

1. Na forma afirmativa, é usada a estrutura: sujeito + *have* + *past participle*.

   In the final round of 2018 championship, our children **have played** together.

   A forma do particípio de verbos regulares é semelhante à do passado simples.

   I **have already studied** a lot because we have a test in a few weeks.

   Para saber a forma do particípio de verbos irregulares, consulte a lista na página 166.

2. Na forma negativa, é usada a estrutura: sujeito + *have not* (*haven't*)/*has not* (*hasn't*) + *past participle*.

   I **haven't written down** everything so far.

3. Na forma interrogativa, é usada a estrutura: *have/has* + sujeito + *past participle* + objeto.

   Have you **talked** to your mom about going out tonight?

◀1 Fill in the gaps using the Present Perfect and the cues in parentheses.

a. She _____ to many different countries, like Thailand and Zimbabwe. (travel – affirmative)

b. _____ they _____ at the same company for 20 years? (work – interrogative)

c. I _____ my History article yet. (write – negative)

d. Katy _____ yet. Traffic must be horrible today. (arrive – negative)

Short answers

Para respostas afirmativas curtas, é usada a estrutura: *Yes* + sujeito + *have/has*. Para respostas negativas curtas, é usada a estrutura: *No* + sujeito + *haven't/hasn't*.

Interrogative			Affirmative			Negative		
Have	I you	been approved in the contest?	Yes,	I you	**have**.	No,	I you	**haven't**.
Has	he she it			he she it	**has**.		he she it	**hasn't**.
Have	we you they			we you they	**have**.		we you they	**haven't**.

Contracted forms

É possível usar a forma contraída do verbo auxiliar *have*.

I/You/We/They have → 've: I**'ve** finally finished my homework.

He/She has → 's: He**'s** bought a brand new laptop.

Time Adverbs

Com o tempo verbal *Present Perfect* são usados *time adverbs* que não expressam um tempo específico.

1. *Ever* é usado com o *Present Perfect* para verificar se até o momento da fala determinada ação já aconteceu. É usado também para fazer perguntas a respeito de experiências.

2. *Already* é usado em afirmativas e interrogativas com o *Present Perfect* para expressar algo que já aconteceu.

3. *Never* é usado em frases afirmativas – ainda que possua um sentido negativo – com o *Present Perfect* para dizer que algo nunca aconteceu.

4. *Yet* é usado em frases negativas com o *Present Perfect* para dizer que algo ainda não aconteceu, mas poderá acontecer no futuro.

5. *Just* é usado com o *Present Perfect* para dizer que algo acabou de acontecer.

2 Complete the sentences using the correct time adverb.

a. I have _____ been to China. I'd love to go there someday.

b. Have you finished your test? I haven't finished it _____.

c. Where are you? I have _____ arrived home and can't find you.

d. Have you _____ eaten Mexican food? No, but I'd like to try it sometime.

e. I have _____ cleaned up my room. Can I play video game now?

UNIT 7

Present Perfect – For and since

Como estudado na unidade 6, o *Present Perfect* é um tempo verbal que expressa ações iniciadas no passado e que ainda estão ocorrendo ou repercutindo no presente.

1. Para indicar o tempo de duração de uma ação no *Present Perfect* é usado *for*.

   for three years   **for** ten days   **for** a minute

2. *Since*, por sua vez, é usado com o *Present Perfect* para indicar quando a ação começou.

   since 1998   **since** this morning   **since** I was a child

◀1 Complete the sentences using **for** or **since**.

   a. My sister has been in the shower _____ 30 minutes now.

   b. I haven't seen my best friend _____ last September.

   c. Diana has been on vacation _____ three years now.

   d. Erica has been taking a nap _____ 3 o'clock.

Present Perfect and Simple Past

Enquanto o *Present Perfect* expressa ações iniciadas no passado e que ainda estão ocorrendo ou repercutindo no presente, o *Simple Past* expressa ações iniciadas e terminadas no passado. Geralmente, as ações descritas pelo *Simple Past* são acompanhadas de frases ou expressões que indicam o tempo em que ocorreram.

I **have traveled** to Nigeria. → **Last month**, I **traveled** to Nigeria.

She **has studied** a lot. → She **studied** a lot **yesterday**.

Active and passive voice

Uma frase escrita ou falada na *active voice* é aquela em que o sujeito da oração é quem realiza a ação. Em língua inglesa essa construção é mais comum do que a *passive voice*.

The famous American author wrote that book.

Na *passive voice*, o sujeito da oração é quem recebe a ação. Essa estrutura é utilizada principalmente quando se quer enfatizar o objeto da ação.

That book was written by the famous American author.

Para formar frases na voz passiva, é usado o verbo *to be* + particípio do verbo principal. Note que a conjugação do verbo *to be* indicará o tempo verbal da frase.

Does the boy **kick** the ball? → **Is** the ball **kicked** by the boy?

My uncle **didn't buy** this new cell phone in New York. → This new cell phone **wasn't bought** by my uncle in New York.

2 Rewrite the sentences from active to passive voice.

a. My mother bakes this strawberry cake every weekend.

_____

b. My best friend sent a message last night.

_____

c. The artist will record a new album.

_____

d. The dog ate all the food.

_____

UNIT 8

First and Second Conditionals

Conditionals são estruturas usadas para expressar condições para algo acontecer ou ter acontecido.

1. A _first conditional_ expressa situações reais e possíveis de acontecer. É usada a estrutura: _If_ + verbo no _Simple Present_, na oração condicional, e _will_ + verbo principal, na oração principal. Assim, a oração no presente expressa uma condição para que a ação principal ocorra.

   If I **finish** these exercises, I **will relax** and **watch** some TV series.

   A _first conditional_ também pode ser usada com _modal verbs_, de acordo com a seguinte estrutura na oração principal: _can/may/must_ + verbo principal.

   If you **eat** the vegetables, you **can have** some ice cream for dessert.

2. A _second conditional_ expressa situações irreais ou improváveis. É usada a estrutura _If_ + _Simple Past_, na oração condicional, e _would_ + verbo principal, na oração principal. Assim, a oração no passado é a condição para que a ação principal ocorra.

   If I **won** the lottery, I **would leave** my job and dedicate myself to humanitarian causes.

   A _second conditional_ também pode ser usada com _modal verbs_ de acordo com a seguinte estrutura na oração principal: _could/should/might_ + verbo principal.

   If I **had** a lot of money, I **could travel** around the world.

1 Complete the sentences using the verbs in parentheses in the first or the second conditionals.

a. If you arrive late for dinner, I _____ angry at you! (be)

b. If it isn't sunny tomorrow, we _____ our picnic. (not have)

c. If Courtney had the money, she _____ the dress we saw at the mall today. (buy)

d. The children _____ bored if they played outside. (not be)

WORKBOOK

NAME: _____

CLASS: _____ DATE: _____

UNIT 1 – AMAZING LANGUAGES

1 Read the comic strip. Then write **T** (true) or **F** (false).

a. ⬭ Each panel shows Garfield's different facial expressions.

b. ⬭ In panel 1, Garfield seems to be bored.

c. ⬭ In the last panel, he seems to be happy.

d. ⬭ Non-verbal language is predominant in the comic strip.

2 Based on the comic strip in activity 1, answer the following questions.

a. What can you infer by looking at Garfield's gestures in the panels 3 to 6?

_____

b. Why did his mood change in the last panel?

_____

3 Complete the jokes using the verbs in parentheses in the appropriate tense.

My three-year-old daughter stuck out her hand and said, "Look at the fly I _____ (kill), Mommy." Since she _____ (eat) a juicy pickle at the time, I thrust her contaminated hands under the faucet and _____ (wash) them with antibacterial soap.

After sitting her down to finish her pickle, I _____ (ask), with a touch of awe, "How _____ you _____ (kill) that fly all by yourself?"

Between bites, she said, "I hit it with my pickle."

A defendant isn't happy with how things _____ (go) in court, so he _____ (give) the judge a hard time.

Judge: Where _____ you _____ (work)?

Defendant: Here and there.

Judge: What _____ you _____ (do) for a living?

Defendant: This and that.

Judge: Take him away.

Defendant: Wait; when _____ I _____ (get out)?

Judge: Sooner or later.

Available at: <www.rd.com/jokes/>. Accessed on: Mar. 24, 2019.

4 Check the best options to complete the sentences.

a. **A:** Do you have _____ questions?

B: I have _____ to ask you. Thank you.

○ some/anything   ○ any/nothing

b. **A:** There is _____ at the door. Can you see who it is?

B: I have already checked. _____ is there, mom.

○ someone/nobody   ○ anyone/nothing

c. Don't tell _____ about _____, right? It's top secret!

○ anyone/anything   ○ someone/something

WORKBOOK

NAME: _____

CLASS: _____ DATE: _____

UNIT 2 – I ENJOY EXTREME SPORTS

1 Read the e-mail below. Then look at the pictures, label the extreme sports they are showing and check the one that Mike did not practice.

To: Sophie

From: Mike

Hi, Sophie! How are you?
I arrived in Switzerland three days ago and you won't believe in everything I have done so far!
The day after my arrival, I practiced snowboarding through the Alps! It was amazing! I also practiced bungee jumping and rafting. I have already scheduled two more adventures for the next three days: skydiving, hang gliding and mountain climbing. I would like to try zorbing, but I have to go back home on Friday. So sad... 🙁
Well, Switzerland really surprised me. I have never thought that this country could offer so many possibilities when it comes to extreme sports. It's a perfect destination for extreme sports lovers like me!
I know you are a sporty person, what about trying some extreme sport with me? Come on, choose one and we will go for it! 😃
I'll call you when I arrive home so we can catch up!
Miss you,
Mike

a.

Salienko Evgenii/Shutterstock

b.

Mny-Jhee/Shutterstock

c.

Sky Antonio/Shutterstock

_____

d.

ChameleonsEye/Shutterstock

e.

onvengradar/Shutterstock

f.

scottshoots/Shutterstock

_____

2 Complete the sentences with the appropriate tag questions.

a. Mike's parents do not approve his preference for extreme sports, _____?

b. You won't give up your dream of practicing bungee jumping, _____?

c. The Bings like their neighbors, _____?

d. Wanda was in trouble last year, _____?

e. I am not late, _____?

3 Complete the dialogs with modal verbs in the affirmative, negative or interrogative form. Then check the true sentences.

a.

> **Can**
>
> **A:** _____ you skateboard, Paul?
>
> **B:** No, I _____. Why?
>
> **A:** Never mind. I want to sell my skateboard so that I _____ buy a new one.
>
> ○ It is an informal situation.   ○ It is a formal situation.

b.

> **May**
>
> **A:** _____ I use your printer, doctor Parker?
>
> **B:** Of course you _____ use it, Steve.
> **A:** Thank you, sir.
>
> ○ In this case, **may** expresses possibility.   ○ In this case, **may** expresses permission.

c.

> **Could**
>
> **A:** _____ you come for a meeting with the vice president tomorrow, Ms. Talbot?
> **B:** Sure. I'll be there.
>
> ○ It is an informal request.   ○ It is a formal request.

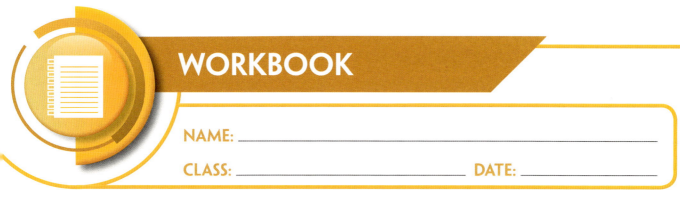

UNIT 3 – YOU MUST TURN YOUR PHONE OFF!

1 Ask two of your friends or family members about how often they do the following activities when they are online. They can answer using the words **rarely**, **sometimes**, or **often**.

How often do you...	Friend or family member #1	Friend or family member #2
send audio messages?		
watch TV series?		
make, edit and post videos?		
play interactive games?		
take and post selfies?		
watch video clips and concerts?		
download apps?		
send text messages?		
chat with friends on social media?		
visit blogs and vlogs?		

Banco de imagens/Arquivo da editora

2 Now, considering the answers given in the previous activity, answer the questions below.

a. What are the differences and similarities between you and your friends/family members when it comes to online habits?

_____

_____

b. Do you think that you and your peers spend too much time online? Why?

_____

_____

3 Complete the cartoon with the words from the box.

you	it	me	my	this

WELCOME TO KINDERGARTEN!

"____'re telling ____ ____ will take 13 years to install ____ education! What kind of outdated software is ____ school using?"

©Glasbergen

GLASBERGEN

4 Let's suppose you are the teacher on the cartoon above and want to advise the boy about education and school. Use the modal verbs **should**, **must** and **mustn't** to write your piece of advice.

_____

_____

_____

5 Complete the dialog below with **can**, **could**, **should** or **would**.

Tom: Did you like the film *A Star is Born*, Vivian?

Vivian: The film is amazing, Tom! You _____ go and see it!

Tom: _____ you like to go with me and watch it again tomorrow?

Vivian: Sure! I _____ meet you in front of the movie theater. I live right beside it!

Tom: _____ you tell me how to get there?

Vivian: Of course! I'll send you the address.

Tom: Thanks! See you.

© Glasbergen/Acervo do cartunista

WORKBOOK

NAME: _____

CLASS: _____ DATE: _____

UNIT 4 – KEEP FIT, KEEP HEALTHY

1 Read the dialog and use the words and expressions from the box to complete it.

> dumbbell weights   equipment   jumping rope   sit-ups
> stretching   treadmill   workout routine

Marcia: Hi, Sandy! You look so healthy! What's the secret?

Sandra: There isn't any! I bought a _____ last year and I decided to walk 40 minutes every day. Of course, I made some healthy changes in my eating habits. Now I eat more fruits and vegetables than any other kind of food.

Marcia: Is the treadmill the only _____ you use?

Sandra: No. I use _____ to build muscle mass.

Marcia: Do you have any routine of exercises?

Sandra: Sure! I love _____ and I also do 60 _____ a day. Before starting my routine, I pull my arms and my legs as much as I can.

_____ is extremely important!

Marcia: I will buy some pieces of fitness equipment and start a _____, too!

Sandra: That's fine, Marcia, but don't forget to talk to a physician before starting to work out, especially if you are not used to exercise regularly, right?

Marcia: Next time we meet, I'll be healthier! Thanks a lot, Sandy!

2 Check the pieces of fitness equipment Sandra uses in her workout routine.

a.
aminphotoz/Shutterstock

b.
MK studio/Shutterstock

c.
Rudy Umans/Shutterstock

d.
New Africa/Shutterstock

3 After some months, Marcia and Sandra met last week. Marcia was healthier and happier. Based on activity 1, write a possible dialog between them.

_____

_____

_____

_____

4 Complete the sentences using the most suitable options from the list below. Use the appropriate relative pronouns to connect the sentences.

> friend has started a workout routine
>
> have unhappy endings
>
> produces pieces of fitness equipment
>
> teaches physical education and athletic training
>
> the teacher is talking to

a. I hate animal movies _____.

b. A P.E. teacher is someone _____.

c. Daniel works for a company _____.

d. Do you know the man _____?

e. We met that woman _____.

5 Check the best alternatives to complete the quotes.

a. We cannot start over. _____ we can begin now _____ make a new ending. (Zig Ziglar, American author)

Available at: <www.openfit.com/20-motivational-quotes-to-help-you-reach-your-fitness-goals>. Accessed on: Mar. 25, 2019.

◯ and/first   ◯ but/and

b. Don't let the scale define _____. Be active, be healthy, be happy." (Unknown author)

Available at: <www.openfit.com/20-motivational-quotes-to-help-you-reach-your-fitness-goals>. Accessed on: Mar. 25, 2019.

◯ you   ◯ me

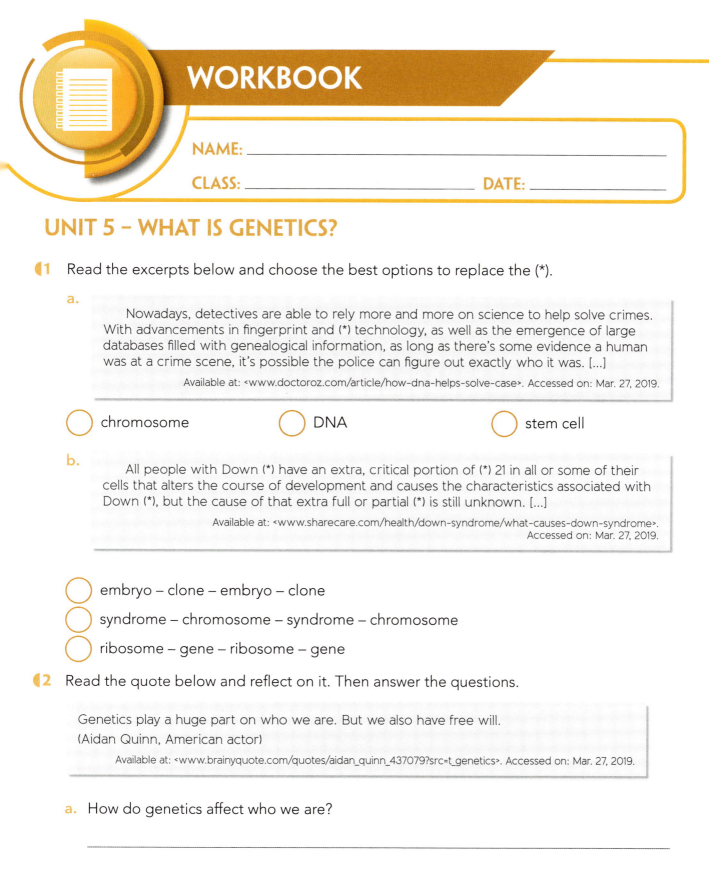

WORKBOOK

NAME: _____

CLASS: _____ DATE: _____

UNIT 5 – WHAT IS GENETICS?

1 Read the excerpts below and choose the best options to replace the (*).

a.

> Nowadays, detectives are able to rely more and more on science to help solve crimes. With advancements in fingerprint and (*) technology, as well as the emergence of large databases filled with genealogical information, as long as there's some evidence a human was at a crime scene, it's possible the police can figure out exactly who it was. [...]
>
> Available at: <www.doctoroz.com/article/how-dna-helps-solve-case>. Accessed on: Mar. 27, 2019.

○ chromosome   ○ DNA   ○ stem cell

b.

> All people with Down (*) have an extra, critical portion of (*) 21 in all or some of their cells that alters the course of development and causes the characteristics associated with Down (*), but the cause of that extra full or partial (*) is still unknown. [...]
>
> Available at: <www.sharecare.com/health/down-syndrome/what-causes-down-syndrome>. Accessed on: Mar. 27, 2019.

○ embryo – clone – embryo – clone

○ syndrome – chromosome – syndrome – chromosome

○ ribosome – gene – ribosome – gene

2 Read the quote below and reflect on it. Then answer the questions.

> Genetics play a huge part on who we are. But we also have free will.
> (Aidan Quinn, American actor)
>
> Available at: <www.brainyquote.com/quotes/aidan_quinn_437079?src=t_genetics>. Accessed on: Mar. 27, 2019.

a. How do genetics affect who we are?

_____

_____

b. What is free will and how can it influence who we are?

_____

_____

3 Read an excerpt of the biography of Mario Capecchi, the Nobel Prize winner in Physiology or Medicine 2007. Complete the text using **a**, **an** or **the**.

⟨ ⟩ www.britannica.com/biography/Mario-Capecchi ___ ⊡ ✕

Mario R. Capecchi

[...]

In _____ 1980s Capecchi began his prize-winning research, which helped give rise to gene targeting. He developed _____ technique using recombinant DNA technology whereby DNA could be injected into _____ nucleus of mammalian cells, greatly enhancing _____ effectiveness of gene transfer. He further refined his procedure, incorporating _____ work of Evans and Smithies into his research, and _____ cooperative effort gave rise to the "knockout mouse"– _____ laboratory mouse in which one or more genes had been selectively inactivated or "knocked out."

Roberto Serra/Iguana Press/Getty Images

Available at: <www.britannica.com/biography/Mario-Capecchi>. Accessed on: Mar. 27, 2019.

4 Complete the dialogs using relative pronouns.

a. **A:** Don't you think that Mr. Geller is such a friendly person?

 B: Mr. Geller?

 A: Yes! That man _____ lives next door.

b. **A:** Hey, Mark! Long time no see!

 B: Hi, Sue. I recently went back to the city _____ I was born. Now I live there!

c. **A:** Who is this person in the photo?

 B: He is doctor Palmer, the scientist _____ researches were rewarded.

5 Write a short paragraph about a person you admire. Use at least four different linking words to express and connect your ideas.

_____

_____

_____

_____

_____

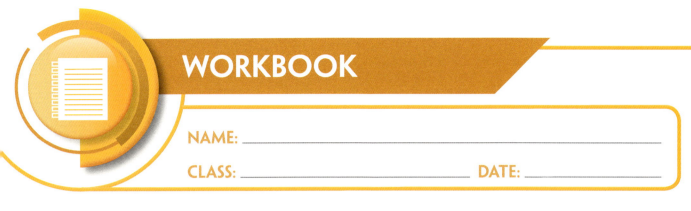

NAME: _____

CLASS: _____ DATE: _____

UNIT 6 – RELATIONSHIPS

1 Read the dialog and look at the picture. Then do the following activities.

Liz: What's up, Carl? I have never seen you so sad!

Carl: Yesterday, I was rude to that boy from the 7th grade.

Liz: Who? Daniel?

Carl: Yes. I was rude to him because of that stupid soccer game.

Liz: What happened?

Carl: Well, he made a mistake during the game. I was so nervous, I yelled at him and called him names. He looked at me so frightened and said nothing. Then he left the court humiliated and silent.

Liz: Oh no, Carl. How could you do that to Daniel? He is such a nice boy...

Carl: I know... Teacher Laura said that I should apologize to him for my terrible behavior.

Liz: I agree. Talk to Daniel and tell him how sorry you are. You'll feel better!

Carl: I'm going to do it right now!

a. Carl is feeling...

◯ unhappy.　　　◯ shocked.　　　◯ glad.　　　◯ anxious.

b. Do you think Carl's attitude towards Daniel should be forgiven? Why (not)?

_____

_____

2 Read the questions and answer them with some of the phrasal verbs from the box below.

break up	cheat on	have a crush on	make up	put up	split up

What are the situations that make you feel...

a. anxious? _____

b. confident? _____

c. embarrassed? _____

3 Imagine that you have a friend, Juan, who lives abroad. Complete the e-mail below telling him about people you both know. Use the pieces of information from the board to write sentences in the Present Perfect.

Liz and Johnny/ decide to get married

Mary/find a new job

aunt Sally/ have a baby

the Greens/ move to New Jersey

Paola/go to South Africa

Post-its: Banco de imagens/Arquivo da editora; Fundo: Africa Studio/Shutterstock

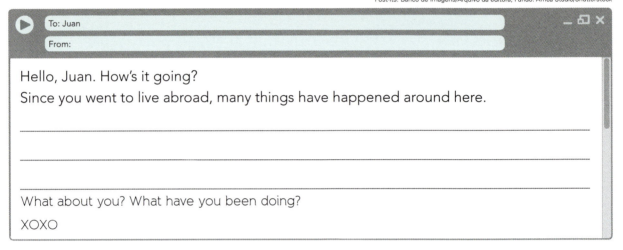

To: Juan

From:

Hello, Juan. How's it going?

Since you went to live abroad, many things have happened around here.

_____

_____

_____

What about you? What have you been doing?

XOXO

4 Answer the questions below. Use the clues in parentheses.

a. **A:** Have you posted the new menu on the restaurant webpage, Tom?
(negative – yet)

   B: I _____, chef.

b. **A:** Have you ever met a famous person?
(negative – never)

   B: Unfortunately, I _____ a famous person.

c. **A:** Has the car broken down?
(positive – already)

   B: Yes. It _____ twice!

d. **A:** Has Cynthia called you lately?
(positive – just)

   B: Yes! She _____ me.

WORKBOOK

NAME: _____

CLASS: _____ DATE: _____

UNIT 7 – THINKING OF GLOBAL ISSUES

1 Read and complete the sentences. Then match them to the appropriate pictures.

a. In 1906, a violent movement of the Earth's surface hit San Francisco.

The _____ was strong and destroyed part of the city.

b. That phenomenal spell of weather was called the Great Heat and came after a stifling

hot summer and long _____.

c. The scale of youth _____ is staggering and shaming.

d. Since 1990 almost 1.1 billion people have escaped extreme _____.

e. Today, there are more than 800 million people who are undernourished. The

_____ is worst in Asia, where about 500 million people don't have
enough food.

f. Did you know air _____ may show up on your face 10 years from now?

2 Check the issues each sentence in activity 1 is related to.

	a	b	c	d	e	f
Social issue						
Environmental issue						

3 In the sentences below, there are some mistakes related to verbs and prepositions. Underline them and rewrite the sentences in the correct form.

a. Hey, Mandy, did you ever study Italian?

_____

b. They have been in South America last year.

_____

c. Margie's parents have known their neighbors since a long time.

_____

d. Marcel lived here for ten years.

_____

e. Jackson has been a doctor at St. Paul General Hospital for 2014.

_____

4 Check the best options to complete the cartoons.

"Your mother and I _____ enough money to send you to any college you like. Would you prefer train or bus?"

○ saved

○ have saved

"My dad is getting old and cranky. Last night at dinner, he _____ the wild rice to settle down."

○ told

○ have told

WORKBOOK

NAME: _____

CLASS: _____ DATE: _____

UNIT 8 – LET'S SAVE OUR PLANET!

1 What do the pictures below refer to? Write **R** for reforestation, **M** for recycling metal, **E** for erosion control, and **W** for wildlife protection.

a.
Hero Images/Getty Images

b.
Steve Kaufman/Corbis NX/Getty Images

c.

Chris Sattlberger/The Image Bank/Getty Images

d.
Liudmila Kotvitckaia/Shutterstock

e.

Michael Snyder/Northwest Florida Daily News/Associated Press/Glow Images

f.
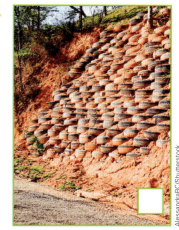
AlessandraRC/Shutterstock

2 Match the fragments to form meaningful sentences.

a. If I met a very famous person,

b. If all my friends come over,

c. If my father were happy with his job,

d. If you tell her my secret,

e. If Mary ate salad as her sister does,

○ he wouldn't seek for another one.

○ I will be mad at you forever!

○ I would ask for a picture and a hug!

○ she would be healthier.

○ my house will be crowded!

3 Complete the sentences below with information about yourself.

a. If I were rich and famous, I _____.

b. If I had enough money, I _____.

c. If I could go back in time, I _____.

d. If I were the president of this nation, I _____.

4 Complete the quotes below using the correct form of the verbs given.

a. **do**

If we all _____ the things we are really capable of doing, we would literally astound ourselves.

(Thomas A. Edison)

Available at: <www.goodreads.com/>. Accessed on: Mar. 31, 2019.

b. **go**

You'll never get anywhere if you _____ about what-iffing like that.

(Roald Dahl, *CHARLIE and the great glass elevator*)

Available at: <www.goodreads.com/>. Accessed on: Mar. 31, 2019.

5 The text below expresses an irony. What do you understand from it?

IMAGINE IF TREES GAVE OFF WI-FI SIGNALS... WE WOULD BE PLANTING SO MANY TREES AND WE'D PROBABLY SAVE THE PLANET TOO. TOO BAD THEY ONLY PRODUCE THE OXYGEN WE BREATHE

AUTHOR UNKNOWN

Reprodução/<www.pinterest.com>

_____

_____

_____

Hello! teens
Readers

Where is Tina?

Asia and Australia

9
STAGE

ELIETE CANESI MORINO
RITA BRUGIN DE FARIA

editora ática

editora ática

Direção Presidência: Mario Ghio Júnior

Direção de Conteúdo e Operações: Wilson Troque

Direção editorial: Luiz Tonolli e Lidiane Vivaldini Olo

Gestão de projeto editorial: Mirian Senra

Gestão de área: Alice Silvestre

Coordenação: Renato Malkov

Edição: Ana Lucia Militello, Carla Fernanda Nascimento (assist.), Caroline Santos, Danuza Dias Gonçalves, Maiza Prande Bernardello, Milena Rocha (assist.), Sabrina Cairo Bileski

Planejamento e controle de produção: Patrícia Eiras e Adjane Queiroz

Revisão: Hélia de Jesus Gonsaga (ger.), Kátia Scaff Marques (coord.), Rosângela Muricy (coord.), Ana Curci, Arali Gomes, Diego Carbone, Gabriela M. Andrade, Luís M. Boa Nova e Patricia Cordeiro

Arte: Daniela Amaral (ger.), Catherine Saori Ishihara (coord.) e Letícia Lavôr (edit. arte)

Diagramação: Mariana Munhato

Iconografia e tratamento de imagem: Sílvio Kligin (ger.), Claudia Bertolazzi (coord.), Célia Rosa (pesquisa iconográfica), Fernanda Crevin (tratamento)

Licenciamento de conteúdos de terceiros: Thiago Fontana (coord.), Flavia Zambon e Angra Marques (licenciamento de textos), Erika Ramires, Luciana Pedrosa Bierbauer, Luciana Cardoso Sousa e Claudia Rodrigues (analistas adm.)

Ilustrações: Igor RAS

Cartografia: Eric Fuzii (coord.), Robson Rosendo da Rocha (edit. arte)

Design: Gláucia Koller (ger.), Talita Guedes (proj. gráfico), Luis Vassallo (capa) e Gustavo Vanini (assist. arte)

Foto de capa: CRS PHOTO/Shutterstock e Uwe Aranas/Shutterstock

---

Todos os direitos reservados por Editora Ática S.A.
Avenida das Nações Unidas, 7221, 3ª andar, Setor A
Pinheiros – São Paulo – SP – CEP 05425-902
Tel.: 4003-3061
www.atica.com.br / editora@atica.com.br

2023
Código da obra CL 742205
CAE 654385 (AL) / 654386 (PR)
8ª edição
4ª impressão
De acordo com a BNCC.

Impressão e acabamento: EGB Editora Gráfica Bernardi Ltda.

Uma publicação **SOMOS** EDUCAÇÃO

NEW DELHI, INDIA

A Good and Cheap Restaurant

Tina: Hi. I'm visiting New Delhi for the first time. Can you recommend some places to visit and give me some information about the city?

Receptionist: Sure! Here! These folders can give you an idea of what the city has to offer.

Tina: Thanks! By the way, is there a good and cheap restaurant near here?

Receptionist: Yes. The Old Delhi, around the corner, is very good.

Tina: Great! Thank you very much.

Receptionist: You're welcome.

🇮🇳 **India**

Capital: New Delhi
Location: South Asia
Area: 3,287,260 sq. km
Population: 1,366,804,917
Currency: Rupee
Languages: Hindi, English and 14 others
Nationality: Indian

New Delhi

Igor RAS/Arquivo da editora

Mapa e bandeira: Banco de imagens/Arquivo da editora

CROSS CULTURAL

In India, besides Hindi and English, there are 14 other languages and about 844 dialects spoken there. It's the second most populous country in the world, with a population of more than one billion people.

Poras Chaudhary/Stone/Getty Images

HOLI FESTIVAL, INDIA.

1 Read and answer the questions.

a. What languages are spoken in India?

_____

b. What is the population of India?

_____

2 Give short answers to the questions.

a. Is Tina in New Delhi? _____

b. Is there a good and cheap restaurant near the hotel? _____

c. Is the restaurant in the hotel? _____

3 Read the text and complete the sentences.

Travelshots/Alamy/Fotoarena

The **tuk-tuk**, or baby taxi, is a motor vehicle. It is a motorized version of a small car with three wheels. The tuk-tuk is a common way of transportation in urban India and can be found in many Asian countries such as Bangladesh, Cambodia, Laos, Pakistan, Sri Lanka and Thailand. It is also found in Guatemala and in some African countries such as Ethiopia and Egypt.

a. The tuk-tuk is a motor _____.

b. You can find tuk-tuks in many countries, such as: India, _____,

_____, _____, _____, _____,

_____, Guatemala, _____ and _____.

SINGAPORE, SINGAPORE

A River Cruise

Tina: Excuse me, can you help me, please?

Tourist: Oh, I can try. I'm a tourist too.

Tina: What else can be done here at the park?

Tourist: Well, you can go on a river cruise. In a bumboat.

Tina: A bumboat?

Tourist: Yeah, that kind of boat over there. It passes through Boat Quay and Clarke Quay.

Tina: It sounds nice.

Tourist: It's very beautiful. I took this cruise yesterday.

Tina: Great. Thank you very much.

Tourist: Enjoy your ride!

Igor RAS/Arquivo da editora

Mapa e bandeira: Banco de imagens/Arquivo da editora

🇸🇬 **Singapore**
Capital: Singapore (city-state)
Location: Southeast Asia
Area: 717 sq. km
Population: 5,858,441
Currency: Singapore dollar
Languages: English, Malay, Chinese, Tamil
Nationality: Singaporean

CROSS CULTURAL

Singapore is a city-state, which means that it is a sovereign nation formed only by a single city and its dependent territories. Another famous city-states are the Vatican City and Monaco.

MARINA BAY, SINGAPORE.

Richie Chan/Shutterstock

1 Correct the information below.

a. Singapore is a country.

_____

b. People speak French in Singapore.

_____

c. Tina will go on a camel ride.

_____

d. The tourist didn't like the river cruise.

_____

2 Read the text and answer the questions.

S-F/Shutterstock

Gardens by the Bay is the perfect place to enjoy the vibrant plant life and escape the city bustle for a moment. Don't miss the **Supertree Grove**, where you can find a cluster of the iconic, futuristic structures that have sustainable functions. Once you spot this wonderful green space you won't be able to stay away.

a. Where can you find the Supertree Grove?

_____

b. What is the Supertree Grove?

_____

3 Read the questions below and discuss them with a classmate.

a. Why is Singapore an eco-friendly city?

b. What sustainable actions are there in your city?

TASMANIA, AUSTRALIA

The Tasmanian Devil

Tour guide: Good morning, everybody!

Tourists: Good morning!

Tour guide: Welcome to Tasmania Island! Before we begin our tour, do you have any questions?

Tina: Excuse me. Could you tell us about the famous "Tasmanian devil"?

Tour guide: The Tasmanian devil is a carnivorous marsupial. Some people believe that there is a giant one living on this mountain and they are afraid of it.

Tina: I've heard incredible stories about it.

Tour guide: People say the devil usually appears during this season so hungry and furious that it grabs all it can find. But I personally...

Tasmanian devil: Huarrrrrrrrrrrrrrr.

Tina: Oh, my god!

Australia
Capital: Canberra
Location: Oceania
Area: 7,741,220 sq. km
Population: 25,047,087
Currency: Australian dollar
Language: English
Nationality: Australian

Tasmania
Island

Mapa e bandeira: Banco de imagens/Arquivo da editora

Igor RAS/Arquivo da editora

CROSS CULTURAL

The Tasmanian devil, a carnivorous marsupial, can only be found in Tasmania. Although it's only the size of a dog, its powerful teeth and jaws (nine times stronger than a dog's and comparable to a shark's or a crocodile's) enable it to devour its prey completely. It looks scary, but the Tasmanian devil only attacks its prey, or when it feels threatened.

Martin Pelanek/Shutterstock

1 Answer the questions.

a. Where can the Tasmanian devil be found?

_____

b. Describe its jaws.

_____

2 Underline the correct words according to the dialog.

a. Some people believe that there is a giant Tasmanian devil living on the **forest/mountain/lake**.

b. The Tasmanian devil is a carnivorous **bird/marsupial/fish**.

3 Read the text and answer the questions.

www.hello!teens.com/cartoonshows _ ⊡ ×

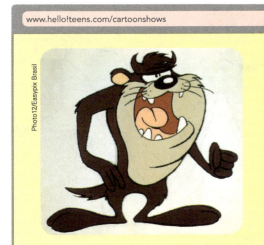

Photo12/Easypix Brasil

Taz-Mania is a cartoon show produced by Warner Bros. Animation. In the year 1991, Taz actually started his own show! This half-hour animated cartoon was about Taz, as an 18-year-old boy with a particular kind of graved gargle known as "Taz-speak". His face was dominated by a mouth ringed with sharp teeth, and the rest of him was shaped like a funnel.

Based on: <http://taz.mientjes.org/>. Accessed on: Mar. 27, 2019.

a. What does Taz look like? Describe him.

_____

_____

b. What is your favorite cartoon character? Describe it.

_____

_____

AUCKLAND, NEW ZEALAND

The Menu, Please!

Tina: Hello! Can I have the breakfast menu, please?

Waiter: Here it is!

Tina: Let me see… Traditional breakfast: bacon, fried mushrooms, sausages, eggs, beans, butter and toast.

Waiter: Here we have the best typical breakfast of New Zealand!

Tina: Oh, it's really delicious, but I'm thinking of having a light breakfast.

Waiter: I suggest our summer breakfast that has tea or coffee, cereal, bread or toast, fresh fruits and fruit juice.

Tina: Ok, I want tea, toast, orange juice, papaya and kiwi.

Waiter: You mean kiwi fruit, of course. New Zealanders are called "Kiwis".

Tina: Kiwis? Why?

Waiter: Our national bird is the Kiwi, a flightless brown bird native of New Zealand. That's where the nickname comes from.

Tina: Oh, how amazing!

Igor RAS/Arquivo da editora

🇳🇿 **New Zealand**
Capital: Wellington
Location: Oceania
Area: 267,710 sq. km
Population: 4,786,708
Currency: New Zealander dollar
Languages: English, Maori
Nationality: New Zealander

Auckland

Mapa e bandeira: Banco de imagens/Arquivo da editora

CROSS CULTURAL

"Taumatawhakatangihangakoauauotama-teaturipukakapikimaungahoronukupokai-whenuakitanatahu", also known as Taumata, is listed in the Guinness World Records as being the longest place's name in the world. It's the name of a hill in Hawke's Bay, in New Zealand. It means "The hill where Tamatea, the man with the big knees, the slider, climber of mountains and land-swallower, played his flute to his loved one".

Wikipedia/Wikimedia Commons

1 What's New Zealand national bird's name?

_____

2 What is "Taumatawhakatangihangakoauauotamateaturipukakapikimaungahoro-nukupokaiwhenuakitanatahu"?

_____

3 Match each word to its meaning.

a. waiter

b. juice

c. New Zealander and American

◯ nationalities

◯ person who serves food and drinks in a restaurant

◯ a refreshing drink

4 Read Tina's dialog again and complete the breakfast menu.

PEARL GARDEN RESTAURANT

Today's Special Breakfasts

Ilustrações: Nik Neves/Arquivo da editora

Traditional breakfast:

_____

_____

_____

Summer breakfast:

_____

_____

_____

MANILA, PHILIPPINES

At the Hairdresser's

Hairdresser: How do you want your hair done, Miss?

Tina: I want it done like Yasmien Meilly's.

Hairdresser: Oh, the actress! She is our customer.

Tina: Really? Does she usually come here?

Hairdresser: Yes, she usually comes here on Saturdays.

Hairdresser: Do you like it this way?

Tina: Yes, it's perfect.

Hairdresser: Do you want some hair spray on it?

Tina: Does Yasmien use it?

Hairdresser: Yes, she does.

Tina: So… yes, please. Yeah! Now I feel like a Filipino movie star!

 Philippines

Capital: Manila
Location: Southeast Asia
Area: 300,000 sq. km
Population: 107,895,139
Currency: Philippine peso
Languages: Filipino, English
Nationality: Filipino

Manila

CROSS CULTURAL

In the Philippines, there are around 50 volcanoes. Mayon Volcano is considered the most active one and had about 58 eruptions until now. Mayon Volcano is well-known for its beauty and near perfect cone – which is a sign of how dangerous it can be. This active volcano is one of the country's tourist attractions.

MAYOR VOLCANO.

Ric Francis/Shutterstock

1 Name one of the Philippines' tourist attractions.

_____

2 Number the sentences according to the dialog.

◯ Tina wants to use hair spray.

◯ Tina wants to look like Yasmien Meilly.

◯ Tina feels like a Filipino movie star.

◯ The hairdresser says that Yasmien Meilly usually goes there.

3 Give short answers to the questions below.

a. Is Tina in Las Vegas?

_____

b. Does Tina want to look like Yasmien Meilly?

_____

c. Is the woman Tina's doctor?

_____

4 Match each word to its meaning.

a. Saturday   ◯ the professional who cuts and styles your hair

b. beauty salon ◯ the day after Friday and before Sunday

c. hairdresser   ◯ the place where people go to get their hair done

5 Complete the sentences according to your own preferences.

a. My favorite actress is _____.

b. My favorite actor is _____.

c. My favorite movie is _____.

d. My favorite singer is _____.

e. My favorite kind of music is _____.

BEIJING, CHINA

What about Visiting the Great Wall?

Tina: Hello! Please, I would like some information about tours in China.

Attendant: Sure. What kind of tours are you thinking about?

Tina: First, I'm planning to visit The Great Wall and perhaps to drift along the Shennong Stream.

Attendant: Oh! It's such a beautiful tour!

Tina: Is it dangerous?

Attendant: No, we have security equipment and instructors that follow all the security rules.

Tina: Great! Can you send me a message with all the directions? I'll call you later.

Attendant: Sure! Where are you staying?

Tina: At The Palace Hotel.

Attendant: OK. Have a great day!

TICKETS

THE GREAT WALL

Igor RAS/Arquivo da editora

Mapa e bandeira: Banco de imagens/Arquivo da editora

 China
Capital: Beijing
Location: East Asia
Area: 9,600,001 sq. km
Population: 1,419,403,920
Currency: Chinese Yuan
Language: Standard Mandarin
Nationality: Chinese

Beijing

CROSS CULTURAL

The Great Wall of China, one of the greatest wonders of the world, is listed as a World Heritage site by Unesco. The Great Wall goes up and down across deserts, grasslands, mountains and plateaus, with approximately 21,196 kilometers from east to west. With more than 2,000 years, some of the sections are now in ruins or have disappeared. In the past, its function was first defensive – to protect the territory against invasions. In the present, it's a symbol of China and a famous tourist attraction.

1 Write **T** (true) or **F** (false), according to the dialog.

a. ◯ Tina wants to go rafting on the Amazon River.

b. ◯ Tina wants to know about tours in Paris.

c. ◯ Tina is going to receive a message in the hotel.

d. ◯ Tina is staying at The Palace Hotel.

2 Match each word to its meaning.

a. directions ◯ a professional who gives the instructions

b. exciting ◯ a lot of fun

c. instructor ◯ to be carried slowly by the water flow

d. drift ◯ instructions to get to a place

3 Fill in the blanks with words from the box.

pictures	believe	anxious	many	place

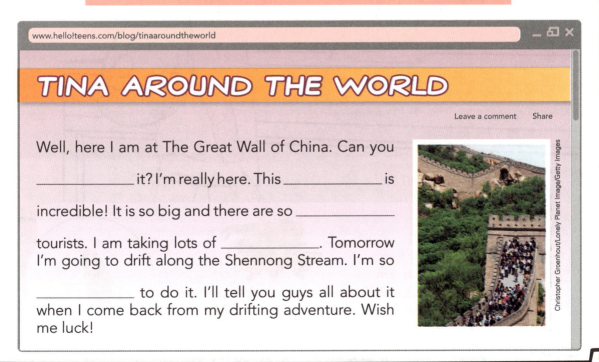

www.hello!teens.com/blog/tinaaroundtheworld

TINA AROUND THE WORLD

Leave a comment   Share

Well, here I am at The Great Wall of China. Can you _____ it? I'm really here. This _____ is incredible! It is so big and there are so _____ tourists. I am taking lots of _____. Tomorrow I'm going to drift along the Shennong Stream. I'm so _____ to do it. I'll tell you guys all about it when I come back from my drifting adventure. Wish me luck!

Christopher Groenhout/Lonely Planet Image/Getty Images

HUALIEN, TAIWAN

A Tour to the National Park

Tina: Excuse me, Miss. Can you help me? I'd like to book a tour to the Taroko National Park.

Clerk: Of course! At the Central Tour Agency you can find many tour options.

Tina: Great! Thanks. I'm going to call the agency.

Clerk: I can call them for you and ask about the tours if you like.

Tina: That's very kind of you! Thank you!

Clerk: It's my pleasure.

Tina: Also, could you please make a reservation for me at the restaurant for 8 p.m.?

Clerk: Of course, Madam.

 **Taiwan**
Capital: Taipei
Location: East Asia
Area: 36,193 sq. km
Population: 23,749,986
Currency: New Taiwan dollar
Languages: Mandarin and Taiwanese
Nationality: Taiwanese

• Hualien

 **CROSS CULTURAL**

LANTERN FESTIVAL, TAIWAN.

kecl/Moment/Getty Images

Taiwan's culture is primarily derived from traditional Chinese culture. The National Palace Museum stores about 700,000 pieces of famous ceramics, sculptures, paintings, porcelain, among other historical objects, in which this influence can be seen. Also, traditional Chinese holidays such as the Chinese New Year, the Lantern Festival and the Dragon Boat Festival are celebrated regularly in Taiwan.

◀1 Answer the questions.

a. What are the traditional Chinese holidays celebrated in Taiwan?

_____

_____

b. What does the National Palace Museum store?

_____

_____

◀2 Read the postcard and fill in the blanks with the words from the box.

dinner	typical	country	everything	friendly	language

Dear Kathy,

Taiwan is such a beautiful _____.
I really have a problem understanding

the _____, but the people are

_____ and the food is delicious here!
Maybe when I get back we can have a

_____ Taiwanese _____

together.

I hope _____ is fine with you.

Your friend,
        Tina

Katherine Heath
3661 Clarkson St.
Denver USA

Dajahof/Shutterstock

17

TOKYO, JAPAN

Would You Like to Join Me?

Tina: Excuse me!

Ted: Hello!

Tina: You were in my Mount Fuji group tour, weren't you?

Ted: Yes, would you like to join me?

Tina: I'd love to. I'm Tina. What's your name?

Ted: I'm Ted. Are you enjoying your trip?

Tina: Yes! I've already traveled to many different countries around the world, but I've never seen such a special culture like this one.

Ted: I feel the same way. This is a really special place. And people here are polite and respectful.

Tina: They sure are!

Ted: Have you already been to a typical restaurant here?

Tina: No, not yet.

Ted: Great! What do you think about having dinner at Choco Kuro at 8 p.m.? On the way there, we can visit Harajuku, a fashion district where we can see gothic, lolita, punk and other styles.

Tina: Yes! Let's go!

🇯🇵 **Japan**

Capital: Tokyo
Location: East Asia
Area: 377,962 sq. km
Population: 126,897,597
Currency: Yen
Language: Japanese
Nationality: Japanese

CROSS CULTURAL

Generally, in Japan, as in many other cultures, the guest takes priority. He or she will be seated in the best place and served the best food and drinks. If staying overnight, the guest will also be offered the first bath (it means the first and clean ofuro's water), and the hosts may even give up their own beds. Also, Japanese people greet each other by bowing, which can be casual or formal, depending on how long and deep it is. Those gestures show that respect is one of Japan's most important values.

1 Read and answer the questions.

a. Were Tina and Ted in the same group tour?

_____

b. What kind of restaurant do Tina and Ted intend to go to?

_____

_____

c. According to Ted, how do people behave in Japan?

_____

_____

d. What examples from the text above confirm Ted's opinion?

_____

_____

2 Match each word to its meaning.

a. enjoying   ◯ something that is not the same

b. restaurant   ◯ to like something very much

c. here   ◯ a place to eat food

d. different   ◯ at this place

3 Read the questions and discuss them with a classmate.

a. How do Japanese people greet each other?

b. How do people greet each other in your country?

c. What other kinds of greetings do you know?

d. In your opinion, which kind of greeting is more popular around the world?

LET'S LEARN MORE ABOUT ASIA AND OCEANIA

Did you know that Asia is the world's largest continent? And that Oceania is the smallest one, considering the landmass?

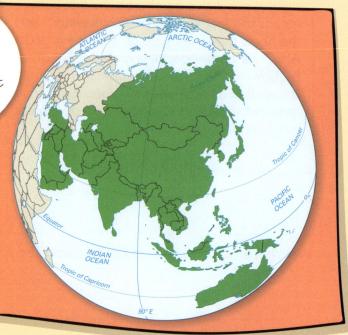

Oceania is the term used to describe one of the 7 continents in order to include the islands surrounding Australia.

It is common to see Australia named as a continent, but this means that all the other islands would not be included in it. Oceania is mostly ocean and spans a vast area.

SYDNEY, AUSTRALIA

There are 14 countries in Oceania: Australia, which is the largest island, Micronesia, Fiji, Kiribati, Marshall Islands, Nauru, New Zealand, Palau, Papua New Guinea, Samoa, Solomon Islands, Tonga, Tuvalu and Vanuatu.

Asia comprises of 48 countries and two of them are also part of the European continent: Russia and Turkey. Russia is the largest country in the Asian continent by landmass, but China is the largest country by population.

There are more than 2,300 recognized languages across Asia and the most spoken one is Chinese.

Let's find out more about some countries in Asia and Oceania!

Some of the most famous tourist attractions in the world can be seen in Asia. They're unique places and people usually include some of them in their bucket lists. But it can be a difficult task to choose one or two among so many beautiful places. Check them out!

PETRA, JORDAN.

Giacomo Terracciano/Shutterstock

MOSCOW, RUSSIA.

Vladimir Zhupanenko/Shutterstock

TAJ MAHAL, AGRA, INDIA.

CRS PHOTO/Shutterstock

BALI ISLAND, INDONESIA.

sembler/Shutterstock

And if you're still in doubt about which one to choose, have a look at what you can find in Oceania!

The Pacific Ocean islands have a tropical vegetation with tropical rainforests. But Australia and New Zealand have varied climatic regions. In Australia, there are rainforests and even deserts! In New Zealand, there are alpine regions with sparse vegetation.

TROPICAL FORESTS, REPUBLIC OF PALAU.

Mike Veitch/Shutterstock

INDIGENOUS ROCK ART, KALUMBURU, AUSTRALIA.

Andrew Atkinson/Shutterstock

The Indigenous rock art in Australia is the oldest in the world. Some aboriginal paintings date back more than 60,000 years and it is still practiced by the indigenous people.

THE SIMPSON DESERT, AUSTRALIA.

Janelle Lugge/Shutterstock

THE SOUTHERN ALPS, NEW ZEALAND.

Linda Kennard/Moment/ Getty Images

In Oceania, you can find platypus and echidna, the only mammals that lay eggs! And speaking of animals, there are more sheep than people in Australia. Kangaroos outnumber humans, too.

FIJI ISLANDS.

David Wall/Danita Delimont/Gallo Images/ Getty Images

PLATYPUS.

Régis Cavignaux/Biosphoto/ Agência France-Presse

ECHIDNA.

anne-tipodees/Shutterstock

Only one-third of the Fijian Islands are inhabited. There are about 300 islands and 540 smaller islets.

INDIA

MUMBAI

Bollywood is the Hindi Film Industry and is located in Mumbai. In the "City of dreams", as Mumbai is called, more than 1,000 films are produced every year. The history of cinema in India dates back to 1913, when the first silent movies were filmed. After that, from sound films, to colored films until the most advanced movies films today, Bollywood is known as the biggest film industry in the world. In the past, Mumbai was called Bombay and then, with the merge of its name with the American Film Industry's, Hollywood, the name Bollywood was formed. In the 1970s, India overtook America as the world's largest film producer and movies can be made in different languages such as Hindi, Urdu and English.

AnilD/Shutterstock

In India, movies are the major source of entertainment, and around 14 million people go to the cinema every day. Cinemagoers pay around a day's wage to watch a movie that usually bring the elements of a good entertainer as music, dance and melodrama.

Based on: <https://www.mumbai.org.uk/mumbai-bollywood.html>. Accessed on: Mar. 27, 2019.

METRO CINEMA, MUMBAI.

❰1 Read the sentences and write **True** or **False**.

a. Bollywood is in America. _____

b. People go to the movies every day in India. _____

c. The cost of a movie ticket can be what a person makes on a day at work. _____

d. Bollywood is bigger than Hollywood. _____

e. Bollywood is in New Delhi. _____

❰2 Match the words to their definitions.

a. cinemagoer   ◯ a language spoken in India

b. Urdu   ◯ a fixed regular payment

c. major   ◯ a person that often goes to the cinema

d. wage   ◯ important

SINGAPORE

SINGAPORE

Known as Singapore's national symbol, the Merlion is a mythical creature with the head of a lion and the body of a fish.

The body symbolizes the humble beginning of Singapore, as a fishing village called Temasek. It means "sea town" in Old Javanese. The head represents the original name of the city, the "lion city" in Malay.

THE MERLION STATUE, SINGAPORE.

S-F/Shutterstock

The statue is a must-see for people visiting Singapore. Visitors today can check on the legend at the Merlion Park, with the statue sprouting water from its mouth in its 8.6 meters and 70 tons. It was originally located at the mouth of the Singapore River, to welcome all visitors to the city. But in 2002 it was relocated to the park, overlooking the Marina Bay.

The Merlion Park also houses a smaller version of the statue, known as the Merlion Cub. It is only 2 meters tall and weighs 3 tons. These are the most well-known among the seven approved Merlion statues in Singapore.

Based on: <https://www.visitsingapore.com/see-do-singapore/recreation-leisure/viewpoints/merlion-park/>.
Accessed on: Mar. 28, 2019.

1 Read the text and find...

a. two animals: _____ .

d. two languages: _____ .

b. the name of a park: _____ .

e. the name of a bay: _____ .

c. the name of a river: _____ .

f. the name of the statue: _____ .

2 Choose the correct answer to complete the sentences.

a. Today, the statue is located in _____ . (Merlion Park/Singapore River)

b. There are _____ approved Merlion statues in Singapore. (two/seven)

c. The statue sprouts water through its _____ . (head/mouth)

AUSTRALIA

QUEENSLAND

One of the seven wonders of the natural world, the Great Barrier Reef is larger than the Great Wall of China and it's the only living thing on Earth that is visible from space. When you see it at distance, you can understand why it is one of the wonders.

It is the largest coral reef of the world and contains an abundance of marine life. It comprises over 3,000 individual reef systems and coral cays and hundreds of picturesque tropical islands. These islands are some of the most beautiful and golden beaches you will find in the world.

The Great Barrier Reef became a touristic destination and visitors can enjoy different experiences as snorkeling, scuba diving, self-sail boats, glass-bottomed boat viewing, cruise ship tours, whale watching and swimming with dolphins. Educational trips to this breathtaking beauty are also available.

Based on: <http://www.greatbarrierreef.org/>. Accessed on: Mar. 28, 2019.

Stringer/Imaginechina/Agência France-Presse

THE GREAT BARRIER REEF, QUEENSLAND.

1 Answer the following questions.

a. What can you find in the Great Barrier Reef?

_____

_____

b. Can the reef be seen from space?

_____

c. Is the reef smaller than the Great Wall of China?

_____

2 Underline the correct information to complete the sentences.

a. The Great Barrier Reef is one of the **ten/seven** wonders of the natural world.

b. The reef is in **Australia/New Zealand**.

c. Visitors can swim with **whales/dolphins** in the sea.

d. Visitors can also **swim/sail** a boat there.

NEW ZEALAND

NORTH ISLAND

If you are a fan of *The Lord of the Rings*, you probably know that the trilogy was filmed all around New Zealand. In the movies, you can see more than 150 real world locations, including Mordor, Hobbiton and Rivendell. There were also soundstages in Wellington, the capital city of the country.

In case you don't have too much time to visit many locations, you can't miss Tongariro National Park. It's New Zealand's oldest park and a world heritage area. It's highlight is Mount Doom (Mount Ngauruhoe is its real name), the place where the famous ring, that names the movie trilogy, was forged. It is an impressing view of a 2,000-year-old mountain peak.

MOUNT NGAURUHOE, NORTH ISLAND.

Tomas Lesa/Shutterstock

You can climb Mount Ngauruhoe but this is not a simple task. It can take you 5 to 6 hours to go to the peak and return to the car park; and the entire cone is made of soft ash. It's like climbing a sand dune! But the view from the top is one of the best you can get in New Zealand.

Based on: <https://www.findingtheuniverse.com/top-three-lord-of-rings-filming/>. Accessed on: Mar. 28, 2019.

1 Complete the sentences with information from the text.

a. The capital city of New Zealand is _____.

b. There are _____ movies in *The Lord of the Rings* series.

c. Tongariro National Park is the country's _____ park.

d. Mount Ngauruhoe's cone is made of soft _____.

e. You can see more than _____ locations from New Zealand in the movie trilogy.

2 Match the numbers to their meaning, according to the text.

a. 5 to 6   ◯ number of different locations used in the movie trilogy

b. 2,000   ◯ number of hours it takes to climb Mount Ngauruhoe

c. 150   ◯ the age of Mount Ngauruhoe

PHILIPPINES

PALAWAN ISLAND

The largest island in the Philippines, Palawan, is half desert. When you visit the island, you can enjoy the jungle, mountains and the beautiful white sand beaches.

Palawan is considered one of the best islands in the world. It is an archipelago with 1,780 islands, known as "the last ecological frontier of the Philippines" due to its landscapes and high biodiversity.

In the north of the island, you can find clear waters, white beaches and many species of fauna and flora. You can also visit El Nido and Taytay, the most famous attractions among tourists. There you can see the limestone cliffs and explore the underwater to see many species of tropical fish and coral, as well as five species of endangered sea turtles. And if you look up, in the jungle, there are around 100 different species of birds!

Based on: <https://www.palawanisland.org/>. Accessed on: Mar. 28, 2019.

EL NIDO, PALAWAN.

Petr Tran/Shutterstock

1 Find in the text the adjectives used to describe the following items.

a. species of birds _____

b. island _____

c. biodiversity _____

d. attractions _____

e. water _____

2 Write **T** (true) or **F** (false).

a. ◯ There are five species of endangered birds in Palawan.

b. ◯ The island is considered one of the best islands in the world.

c. ◯ There are around 100 species of fish in the island.

d. ◯ El Nido and Taytay are the most famous tourist attractions in Palawan.

CHINA

CHENGDU

Something you can see in China but nowhere else is a center for giant pandas. One of the most popular destinations for tourists in Chengdu is the Giant Panda Breeding Research Base (or Chengdu Panda Base) that specializes in baby pandas and their care. There, you can see 50 giant pandas in a half-day visit. You can also learn more about them in the museum and even see a baby panda!

But don't expect a zoo-like atmosphere. The place is a research center, so it does not focus on displaying animals. Their focus is on taking care of breeding pandas and, also, on providing interactive activities that teach people about pandas and their protection.

Uwe Aranas/Shutterstock

When visiting the center in cool weather, you'll probably see the giant pandas outdoors. You don't need a map to walk around the center and you can easily find out where the giant pandas are by just following the noise of visitors. Whenever there is a panda walking, climbing on a tree, eating bamboo or even sleeping, there is noise from people amazed at these enchanting creatures.

Based on: <https://www.chinahighlights.com/chengdu/attraction/panda-breeding-and-research-center.htm>. Accessed on: Mar. 28, 2019.

THE GIANT PANDA BREEDING RESEARCH BASE, CHENGDU.

1 Read and answer the questions according to the text.

a. Where can giant pandas be found in Chengdu?

_____

_____

b. How many giant pandas can be seen in a half-day visit to the center?

_____

_____

c. What are the objectives of this research center?

_____

_____

2 Underline the correct answer.

a. There are **fifty/sixty** giant pandas in Chengdu Panda Base.

b. You can see pandas outdoors in **cool/warm** weather.

c. There is a **theater/museum** at the center.

d. The center **is/isn't** like a zoo.

TAIWAN

TAIPEI

Taiwan, formerly also known as Formosa, is the main island of the Republic of China (Nationalist China). Located 185 km (115 miles) off the southeast coast of mainland China [...].

As presently constituted, the Republic of China includes the island of Taiwan; 15 nearby islands that are part of the Taiwan group; 64 small islands in the Pescadores (Penghu Islands); and the strategically important islands of Quemoy and Matsu near the mainland coast. Taiwan was modernized during the period of Japanese control and since 1949 has developed one of the world's fastest-growing industrial and export-oriented economies. [...]

The major products include electronics equipment, textiles, chemicals, clothing, processed foods, ships, and such traditional handicrafts as ceramics, silks, and bamboo and paper items. [...]

Available at: <http://go.grolier.com/print?id=0283210-0&type=0ta&product_id=gme&authcode=gme>. Accessed on: Mar. 28, 2019.

Arunporn Thanapotivirat/Shutterstock

TAIPEI SKYLINE.

1 Answer the questions.

a. Which is the main island of the Republic of China?

_____

b. What is the other name of Taiwan?

_____

c. What did Taiwan develop after 1949?

_____

2 Write the name of Taiwan's major products next to their definition.

a. Articles made by shaping pieces of clay: _____.

b. Electronical inventions made for a particular purpose: _____.

c. Any cloth produced by weaving, knitting, or felting: _____.

d. Vessels made for transporting goods or people by sea: _____.

e. Garments used to cover a person's body: _____.

JAPAN

HIROSHIMA AND NAGASAKI

Japan is a country from East Asia, which consists of four main islands and a few thousand smaller islands in the western North Pacific Ocean. Japan has one of the highest population number among other countries, and its capital, Tokyo, is one of the world's largest cities.

As Japan is situated in a volcanic zone along the Pacific deeps, there are frequent low intensity earth tremors and occasional volcanic activity throughout the islands. Destructive earthquakes occur several times a century, often resulting in tsunamis.

During World War II, on December 7, 1941, Japan attacked the American naval base in Pearl Harbor and declared war against the United States. As a counterattack, the North American country sent nuclear bombs to the Japanese cities Hiroshima and Nagasaki which devastated them completely. Nevertheless, Japan went through a process of reconstruction and in the late 20th century it had already become one of the world's most developed countries.

Japanese history is a living example of restoration, development and discipline. In less than 150 years, Japan went from an isolated feudal state to a powerful country and shows us nowadays a mix of high technology with traditional culture and values.

Based on: <http://kids.britannica.com/comptons/article-9275136/Japan>. Accessed on: Mar. 28, 2019.

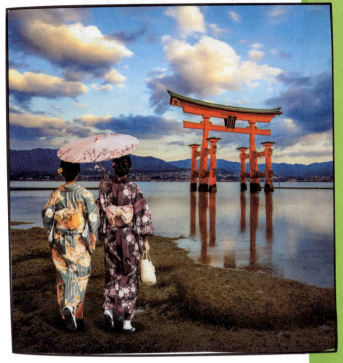

Pajor Pawel/Shutterstock

FLOATING TORII GATE AT MIYAJIMA, HIROSHIMA.

◀1 Answer the following questions.

a. What are the historical facts that took place in the 20th century mentioned in the text?

_____

b. How long did the development of Japan from a feudal state to a powerful country take?

_____

c. What does the Japanese history show us?

_____

◀2 Search on the Internet and write a short paragraph about the fields of technology Japan is famous for.

_____

_____

_____

_____

GLOSSARY

A

a lot of: muito
aboriginal: aborígene
about: aproximadamente; sobre
abundance: abundância
according: de acordo
across: de um lado para o outro
act: ato
active: ativo/a
activity: atividade
actor: ator
actress: atriz
actually: na verdade
advanced: avançado/a
afraid: ter medo
after: depois
age: idade
all: todo
along: ao longo de
alpine: alpino
already: já
also: também
although: embora
amazing: incrível
among: entre
amusing: divertido/a
animated: animado/a
another: outro
answer: responder
anxious: ansioso/a
appear: surgir, aparecer
approve: aprovar
approximately: aproximadamente
archipelago: arquipélago
around: ao redor, em torno de
arrive: chegar
art: arte
article: artigo
as well as: assim como
ash: cinza
at least: pelo menos
atmosphere: ambiente; clima
attack: atacar
attendant: atendente
attraction: atração
available: disponível

B

bamboo: bambu
barrier: barreira
bath: banho
bay: baía
be able: ser capaz de
beach: praia

bean: feijão
beautiful: bonito/a
beauty: beleza
become: tornar-se
bed: cama
before: antes
beginning: início, começo
believe: acreditar
below: abaixo
besides: além de
best: melhor
big: grande
billion: bilhão
bird: pássaro
boat: barco
body: corpo
bow: fazer uma reverência
bread: pão
breakfast: café da manhã
breathtaking: deslumbrante
breeding: criação; reprodução
bring: trazer
bustle: agitação
but: mas
butter: manteiga
by the way: a propósito

C

call: ligar; chamar
camel: camelo
can: poder; ser capaz de
care: cuidado
carnivorous: carnívoro
carry out: pôr em prática
cartoon: desenho animado
cay: ilhota de coral
celebrate: comemorar
century: século
ceramic: cerâmica
character: personagem
cheap: barato
check: verificar
chemicals: substâncias químicas
cinemagoers: frequentadores de cinema
city: cidade
clean: limpo; claro
clerk: atendente
cliff: penhasco
climatic: climático
climb: escalar; subir
cloth: tecido
clothing: vestuário
cluster: agrupamento
coast: costa
coffee: café
colored: colorido/a
common: comum

comparable: comparável
completely: completamente
comprise: formar
consequence: consequência
consider: considerar
considering: levando em conta
consist: consistir em algo
constitute: constituir
contain: conter
cool: frio
corner: esquina
correct: corrigir
cost: custo
counterattack: contra-ataque
country: país
creature: criatura
cricket: críquete
crocodile: crocodilo
crop: cultura
cruise: cruzeiro
culture: cultura
curiosity: curiosidade
currency: moeda

D

dance: dança
dangerous: perigoso/a
date: datar
declare: declarar
deep: profundo/a
defensive: defensivo/a
delicious: delicioso/a
density: densidade
dependent: dependente
derive: obter algo de algo
describe: descrever
desert: deserto
destination: destino
destructive: destrutivo/a
devastate: devastar
develop: desenvolver
development: desenvolvimento
devil: demônio
devour: devorar
dialect: dialeto
different: diferente
dinner: jantar
direction: direção
disappear: desaparecer
discipline: disciplina
discuss: discutir, debater
display: expor
distance: distância
district: distrito
doctor: médico/a
dolphin: golfinho
dominate: dominar

dragon: dragão
dream: sonho
drifting: tipo de passeio em rio utilizando pequeno barco
drink: bebida
during: durante

E

each: cada
earthquake: terremoto
easily: facilmente
east: leste
eat: comer
Earth: Terra (planeta)
echidna: equidna
ecological: ecológico
economy: economia
educational: educacional
egg: ovo
electronic: eletrônico
element: elemento
else: mais
enable: possibilitar
enchanting: encantador
endangered: ameaçado de extinção
engine: motor
enjoy: curtir, gostar
entertainer: animador/a
entertainment: entretenimento, diversão
entire: inteiro, todo
equipment: equipamento
eruption: erupção
escape: escapar
even: até; mesmo
every: todo
everybody: todos
everything: tudo
example: exemplo
exciting: empolgante
expect: esperar
experience: experimentar
explore: explorar
export: exportar

F

face: rosto
famous: famoso/a
fan: fã
fashion: moda
favorite: favorito/a
feel: sentir
few: algum
field: campo
film: filmar; filme
find: encontrar

find out: descobrir (algo)
first: primeiro/a
fish: peixe
fishing: pesca
flightless: não voador/a
focus: foco da atenção
folder: pasta
follow: seguir
food: comida
footwear: calçado
forest: floresta
forge: forjar
form: formar
formerly: anteriormente
frequent: frequente
fried: frito/a
friendly: amigável, simpático/a
frontier: fronteira
fruit: fruta
fun: diversão
function: função
funnel: funil
furious: furioso/a
futuristic: futurista

garden: jardim
garment: peça de roupa
generally: em geral
giant: gigante
give: dar
give up: deixar (algo); desistir
go: ir
go through: passar por algo
golden: dourado/a
good: bom/boa
grab: agarrar
grassland: pradaria
great: ótimo/a
green: verde
greet: cumprimentar
greeting: saudação
group: grupo
grove: pomar
growing: crescente
guest: convidado/a
guide: guia
guy: cara

hair: cabelo
hairdresser: cabeleireiro/a
hairdresser's: salão de cabeleireiro
half: meio, metade
handicraft: artesanato
have: ter
head: cabeça
hear: ouvir
help: ajudar
here: aqui

heritage: patrimônio
high: alto
highlight: destaque
hill: colina
historical: histórico/a
holiday: feriado
host: anfitrião
hour: hora
how: como
humble: humilde
hundred: centena
hungry: com fome

icon: ícone
iconic: icônico/a
impressing: impressionante
in case: caso
in order to: para, a fim de
include: incluir
incredible: incrível
incredibly: incrivelmente
indigenous: indígena
industry: indústria
inhabited: habitado/a
instructor: instrutor
intend: pretender
intensity: intensidade
interactive: interativo/a
into: dentro de
invention: invenção
island: ilha
islet: pequena ilha
isolated: isolado/a

jaw: mandíbula
join: juntar
juice: suco
jungle: selva

kangaroo: canguru
kind: tipo
knee: joelho
knitting: tricô
know: saber; conhecer

lady: senhora
lake: lago
landmass: continente
land-swallower: pessoa que viaja longas distâncias por terra
language: idioma
lantern: lanterna

large: grande
largest: o maior
lay: pôr, colocar
lead: conduzir
learn: aprender
legend: lenda
life: vida
like: gostar
limestone: calcário
lion: leão
list: lista; listar
live: morar
living: vivo
lobby: saguão
location: localização; posição
look: olhar
look like: parecer com algo/ alguém
lord: senhor
low: baixo

mainland: continental
major: principal
make: fazer
mammal: mamífero
many: muito
marine: marinho
may: poder
mean: significar
meet: encontrar
menu: cardápio
merge: unir(-se)
meter: metro
mile: milha
miss: sentir falta
mix: mistura
modernize: modernizar(-se)
moreover: além disso
mostly: principalmente
mountain: montanha
mouth: boca
movie: filme
museum: museu
mushroom: cogumelo
music: música
mythical: mítico

nation: nação
nationality: nacionalidade
near: perto
nearby: próximo/a
need: precisar
never: nunca
nevertheless: no entanto
nice: agradável
nickname: apelido
nine: nove
noise: barulho
north: norte
now: agora

nowadays: hoje em dia
nowhere: em nenhum lugar
number: numerar

occasional: esporádico/a
occur: ocorrer
ocean: oceano
of course: certamente
off: distante
offer: oferecer
often: frequentemente
oldest: o/a mais velho/a
once: uma vez
one-third: um terço
only: somente
option: opção
orange: laranja
other: outro/a
outdoor: ao ar livre
outnumber: exceder em número
over: acima de, sobre
overlook: dar para (vista)
overnight: durante a noite
overtake: ultrapassar
own: próprio/a

painting: pintura
papaya: mamão
paper: papel
park: parque
past: passado
pay: pagar
peak: pico
pearl: pérola
people: pessoas; povo
perfect: perfeito/a
perhaps: talvez
personally: pessoalmente
picture: fotografia
picturesque: pitoresco/a
piece: peça
place: lugar
plan: planejar
plant: planta
plateau: planalto
platypus: ornitorrinco
please: por favor
pleasure: prazer
population: população
porcelain: porcelana
postcard: cartão-postal
powerful: poderoso/a
practice: praticar
preference: preferência
presently: no momento
prey: presa
primarily: principalmente
priority: prioridade

probably: provavelmente
process: processo
produce: produzir
protection: proteção
provide: suprir
purpose: propósito

quay: cais

rainforest: floresta tropical
rank: posto
read: ler
reader: leitor/a
really: realmente
receive: receber
recepcionist: recepcionista
reconstruction: reconstrução
reef: recife
refreshing: refrescante
region: região
regularly: regularmente
related: relacionado/a
relocate: transferir
represent: representar
require: exigir
research: pesquisa
reservation: reserva
rest: resto
restaurant: restaurante
restoration: restauração
result: resultar
return: voltar
ride: viagem
ring: anel
river: rio
rock: pedra
ruin: ruína
rule: regra

sail: velejar; vela
same: mesmo/a
sand: areia
Saturday: sábado
sausage: salsicha
say: dizer
scuba diving: mergulho
(usando tubo de oxigênio)
sculpture: escultura
sea: mar
sea turtle: tartaruga marinha
season: estação do ano
seat: sentar
second: segundo/a
section: seção
security: segurança
see: ver
self-sufficient: autossuficiente

send: enviar
serve: servir
seven: sete
several: vários
shaped: com forma de
shark: tubarão
sharp: afiado
sheep: ovelha
ship: navio
short: curto/a
show: mostrar; programa
silent: mudo/a, calado/a
silk: seda
since: desde
single: único
situation: situação
size: tamanho
slider: aquele/a que desliza
small: pequeno/a
snorkeling: mergulho (usando
snorkel)
so: tão
soccer: futebol
soft: macio, suave
some: alguns
something: alguma coisa, algo
sound: soar; som
source: fonte
south: sul
southeast: sudeste
southern: do sul
sovereign: soberano/a
space: espaço
sparse: escasso/a
speak: falar
specialize: especializar
species: espécie
sport: esporte
spot: identificar
sprout: brotar
start: começar
state: estado
statue: estátua
stay: ficar
stay away: ficar distante
still: ainda
stomach: estômago
store: armazenar
story: história
strategically:
estrategicamente
strong: forte
structure: estrutura
style: estilo
such as: por exemplo
suggest: sugerir
summer: verão
Sunday: domingo
sure: claro, certamente
surrounding: nos arredores
sustainable: sustentável
swallow: engolir
swim: nadar
symbol: símbolo
symbolize: simbolizar

take: pegar
take care: cuidar de
tall: alto
task: tarefa
tea: chá
teach: ensinar
teeth: dentes
tell: dizer
tenth: décimo
term: termo
territory: território
text: texto
textile: tecido; têxtil
there is/are: há
there were: havia
these: estes
thing: coisa
think: pensar
this: este/a
thousand: mil
threatened: ameaçado/a
throughout: por toda a parte
ticket: ingresso
time: tempo
toast: torrada
ton: tonelada
too much: muito/a
tour: viagem, excursão
tourist: turista
town: cidade; centro
toy: brinquedo
traditional: tradicional
travel: viajar
trilogy: trilogia
trip: viagem
try: tentar
tuk-tuk: veículo pequeno de
três rodas usado como táxi em
alguns países do mundo
typical: típico/a

underline: sublinhar
understand: entender
underwater: subaquático/a
until: até
urban: urbano/a
use: usar
usually: geralmente,
normalmente

value: valor
varied: variado/a
vast: vasto/a
vegetation: vegetação
vehicle: veículo
version: versão

very: muito
vessel: embarcação
vibrant: vibrante
view: vista
village: vila
visible: visível
visit: visitar
visitor: visitante
volcanic: vulcânico
volcano: vulcão

wage: salário
wait: esperar
waiter: garçom
walk: andar
wall: muro, parede
want: querer
war: guerra
warm: quente
watch: assistir
water: água
way: forma, maneira
weather: clima
weave: tecer
weigh: pesar
welcome: dar as boas-vindas
well: bem
well-known: conhecido/a
west: oeste
western: do oeste
whale: baleia
what: que
wheel: roda
whenever: sempre que/
quando
where: onde
which: qual
white: branco/a
whose: de quem
why: por que; por quê
with: com
wonder: maravilha
wonderful: maravilhoso/a
work: trabalho
write: escrever

year: ano
yesterday: ontem
yet: já
yogurt: iogurte
you're welcome: de nada

zone: área; zona
zoo: zoológico